Retiring with Purpose

Retiring with Purpose

A Practical Guide to Planning a Flexible and Meaningful Retirement

TRICIA RYAN SNOW

ROCKRIDGE
PRESS

For general information on our other products and services or to obtain technical support, please contact our Customer Care Department within the United States at (866) 744-2665, or outside the United States at (510) 253-0500.

Rockridge Press publishes its books in a variety of electronic and print formats. Some content that appears in print may not be available in electronic books, and vice versa.

Interior and Cover Designer: Brian Lewis
Art Producer: Tom Hood
Editor: Reina Glenn
Production Manager: Michael Kay
Production Editor: Melissa Edeburn

Illustrations © Wesley Valenzuela, 2020. Author photograph courtesy Katherine Wilson.

ISBN: Print 978-1-64876-611-4
eBook 978-1-64739-899-6
R0

This book is dedicated to the followers of my blog, baby boomers, and Gen Xers who are looking to live their best lives during retirement.

Contents

Introduction

The year was 2008, and the United States was spiraling into financial meltdown. We had all our eggs in real estate and banking, and I watched as we lost everything we had worked for.

Why had I thought these investments were two separate baskets? What had convinced me if one industry failed, the other would sustain us? We went from being millionaires to owing the banks more than $1.5 million, with assets that had depreciated over 60 percent. My net worth dropped from $1 million to zero in a matter of months.

I had worked primarily in the mortgage industry through-out the previous decade, and I had no idea what I was going to do moving forward. How could I not have seen this situation coming?

The truth was I had seen it coming; I'd just never thought it would get as bad as it did. We had stopped buying property from 2004 to 2007 during the real estate boom, knowing the market would correct itself, and we had tried to prepare. I'd patiently waited while other folks continued scooping up and flipping properties, knowing the real estate industry was a house of cards that could tumble. I thought I'd played it safe, but I couldn't have imagined what the 2007 financial crisis would do to us or our nation. It was a scary time.

In an instant, retirement seemed out of the question. How would we ever rebuild in time? Was there any hope? The debt was overwhelming, and the banking industry was in total chaos.

To survive, we had to think outside the box. We still had our real estate investments, so my husband started a property management business to continue managing our rentals. I was able to get a decent-paying job and made my way back to banking as a retail branch manager. It was an environment in which I thrived. I was happy in my role, and I had five successful years.

Then I got a new boss. Then another. The bank I worked for began to shut down branches and regularly cut staff. The new management was toxic and alienating. I was miserable.

Within six months, the work started to take a toll on my health. Could I live this way for the next 15 years? Would it be the same situation somewhere else? Could I retire now?

I ended up in urgent care with a pounding heart. As I had suspected, the diagnosis was anxiety, something I had never dealt with. Living this way was no longer an option. I knew I needed to leave banking, but for what?

The time to reinvent myself again had arrived, but this time, I decided to craft the life my husband and I wanted to start living now. I did not want to wait for retirement.

In fact, my idea of retirement had completely changed. I started asking myself new questions: What would a retirement lifestyle look like with our current finances? Did I really want to stop working and play tennis every day? Was I going to wait until my sixties to travel the world? What was I moving toward in my life?

I needed to answer all these questions before deciding the direction I would take, and these questions are where you should start, too.

How to Use This Book

The questions this book will ask about your finances, interests, and personal goals will drive you to seriously analyze your current realities. Numerous exercises will help you visualize not only your current priorities but also the ways your intentions might grow and change during retirement. The overall goal of this book is to give you the tools to create a retirement that maximizes fulfillment while balancing leisure and purpose.

Write your answers directly into this book, if you'd like, but be sure to keep a journal nearby to jot down ideas as you go through the exercises and let them guide your visualizations toward a solid plan.

Remember, there are no right or wrong answers. This journey is yours, and no matter your current situation, you can create a retirement lifestyle on your terms based on your dreams and vision.

Part I

Knowing Where You Are

You have likely thought about what your retirement will look like, but do you understand what you need to do to get there? Consider the self-inventory exercises in this part of the book to be the first steps toward determining your wants and needs in retirement and understanding your current realities.

CHAPTER 1

Money Matters

Most Americans spend more time planning their vacations than they do their retirement. Maybe that's because the prospect seems daunting, but retirement planning isn't so different from tackling other life goals—you have to start where you are now. Your vision may change over time, but no matter where you end up, the beginning of your retirement planning should be assessing how well your current financial situation can fund your desired lifestyle. This chapter will help you examine your timelines, calculate your after-tax income, determine your risk tolerance, and come up with a plan for your estate.

Busting Retirement Myths

Advice on the internet about how to fund retirement is mainly divided between financial advisors, who believe you can't save too much and don't recommend relying on the government, pensions, or part-time work; and retirement blogs, which say retirees don't need as much income as they think, everyone is working in retirement now, mortgages don't have to be paid off, and government funding is stable. So which is correct?

The answer is both! The biggest myth about retirement is that it should look the same for everyone. Here are some other common myths about retirement with explanations for why they may not be true for you:

Myth: You'll have higher medical and lifestyle expenses during retirement, so you should try to have the same income when you retire as when working.

Fact: Expenses are usually lower in retirement because you have options like downsizing or moving to an area that offers a lower cost of living. You will no longer be commuting to work, and expenses like dry cleaning and even clothing budgets are significantly lower in retirement.

Myth: Medicare will take care of all your health care expenses.

Fact: Depending on your income and tax status, you may still have to pay a premium for Medicare. You will also have co-pays and out-of-pocket expenses.

Myth: Retirement is short.

Fact: Seniors are living longer than ever. With the average retirement age at 65 and average life expectancy around 80, retirement is often at least 15 years.

Retirement is different for everyone because countless factors determine what an individual's retirement will look like, and situations can evolve over the years. Working part-time during retirement is a necessary reality for many Americans, but others will continue to work simply because they want to.

Here, we will go over the factors you need to consider to determine your financial situation in retirement, which will, in turn, give you an idea of whether you should continue to work. You may start off working part-time and transition into full-time leisure—everyone comes from different places and time frames as they approach retirement.

Figuring Out What You Need

If you do not understand your financial situation, it will be difficult to know what plans you can make for retirement. You probably know how much money you've saved for retirement, but you may not know whether it will be enough to allow you to live comfortably once you retire. Remember that the values of your current IRAs and 401(k)s are likely to continue increasing as you approach retirement. So if you're 20 years from retirement, the amount you currently have in these accounts will likely be significantly more than what they are now. AARP has a helpful 401(k) calculator tool to help you get a sense of the predicted value (see "AARP" in Resources, page 148).

Here are some practical steps to make sense of your finances:

Evaluate Your Monthly Expenses

According to most retirement planners, you will need eight times your salary for a 25-year retirement. For example, if you are earning $80,000 per year when you retire at age 67, you will need at least $640,000 in your nest egg.

Another way to consider how much you'll need to have saved is to assume you will need 70 to 80 percent of your income for retirement. So if you were making $100,000 per year, you would need $70,000 to $80,000 per year to live comfortably in retirement.

Use this worksheet to list your monthly expenses now as well as your projected expenses in retirement. If you aren't sure what your retirement expenses will look like yet, just list your current figures.

Personal Monthly Budget

CURRENT MONTHLY INCOME	Income 1	
	Extra income	
	Total monthly income	

PROJECTED MONTHLY RETIREMENT INCOME	Income 1	
	Extra income	
	Total monthly income	

HOUSING	Current Cost	Projected Cost in Retirement	Difference
Mortgage or rent			
Phone			
Electricity			

HOUSING	Current Cost	Projected Cost in Retirement	Difference
Gas			
Water and sewer			
Cable			
Waste removal			
Maintenance or repair			
Supplies			
Other			
SUBTOTAL			

TRANSPORTA- TION	Current Cost	Projected Cost in Retirement	Difference
Vehicle payment			
Bus/taxi fare			
Insurance			
Licensing			
Fuel			
Maintenance			
Other			
SUBTOTAL			

INSURANCE	Current Cost	Projected Cost in Retirement	Difference
Home			
Health			
Life			
Other			
SUBTOTAL			

FOOD	Current Cost	Projected Cost in Retirement	Difference
Groceries			
Dining out			
Other			
SUBTOTAL			

PETS	Current Cost	Projected Cost in Retirement	Difference
Food			
Medical			
Grooming			
Toys			
Other			
SUBTOTAL			

PERSONAL CARE	Current Cost	Projected Cost in Retirement	Difference
Medical			
Hair/nails			
Clothing			
Dry cleaning			
Health club			
Organization dues or fees			
Other			
SUBTOTAL			

ENTERTAINMENT	Current Cost	Projected Cost in Retirement	Difference
Video/DVD			
CDs			
Movies			
Concerts			
Sporting events			
Live theater			
Other			
Other			
Other			
SUBTOTAL			

LOANS	Current Cost	Projected Cost in Retirement	Difference
Personal			
Student			
Credit card			
Credit card			
Credit card			
Other			
SUBTOTAL			

TAXES	Current Cost	Projected Cost in Retirement	Difference
Federal			
State			
Local			
Other			
SUBTOTAL			

SAVINGS OR INVESTMENTS	Current Cost	Projected Cost in Retirement	Difference
Retirement account			
Investment account			
Other			
SUBTOTAL			

GIFTS AND DONATIONS	Current Cost	Projected Cost in Retirement	Difference
Charity 1			
Charity 2			
Charity 3			
SUBTOTAL			

LEGAL	Current Cost	Projected Cost in Retirement	Difference
Attorney			
Alimony			
Payments on lien or judgment			
Other			
SUBTOTAL			

CURRENT BALANCE (CURRENT INCOME MINUS CURRENT EXPENSES)	
RETIREMENT BALANCE (PROJECTED INCOME MINUS PROJECTED EXPENSES)	
DIFFERENCE (CURRENT MINUS PROJECTED)	

If your current numbers came out in a deficit, you can take several steps now to adjust your finances for the future. It's important not to become fearful or panicky. For many, "planning" continues well into retirement as you adapt your finances to your new way of life.

Let's go over the different ways you can shift your expectations if you feel you do not have enough financial security to retire.

Evaluate Your Assets

You might not have realized it, but while you were listing your expenses in the budget sheet, you were also documenting your assets. Rearranging your assets (like property and investments) is a common practice as you approach retirement to potentially capitalize on a better return. Here are some assets to consider:

> **Investments:** You may still have the same investments you chose when you were first setting up your 401(k), and they might not be the best options for you now. Ask your financial advisor to evaluate your current investments. Is there something you could be doing differently that might bring a better return? Investigate other investment options to help reach your goals.
>
> Here are some key points to remember:
>
> ▸ Make sure you are rebalancing your portfolio often. Funds can underperform after time, so check on how they are doing and evaluate your portfolio annually.
>
> ▸ Check the fees. Are there similar returns on investments with fewer or smaller fees?
>
> ▸ If you do not have a financial advisor, start looking for one now. Even if your 401(k) is your only

investment account, someone will have to manage those funds when you retire. Interview advisors now and have them help you with your current strategy and check the performance of your existing retirement funds. Find out what investment strategy they recommend for when you retire and what you should expect from your investments during retirement.

Real Estate: Are you in a home that can be downsized? Do you have a vacation home that can create income or be sold so the proceeds can be invested? Once our kids were on their own, we evaluated our home and realized it was more than we needed for our lifestyle and had maintenance issues that were becoming overwhelming as we aged. By downsizing, we were able to pay down remaining debt on our other homes and free up additional income and time. That shift enabled us to live the retirement lifestyle we wanted.

Here are some simple steps to determine if downsizing is the right choice for you:

- Meet with a realtor to learn your home's value in the current market.

- Consider any foreseeable fluctuations in your home's property value. Are you in a hot real estate market? Is it expected to continue rising in the next few years?

- Compare your current expenses, such as utilities, homeowners' insurance, and property taxes, with those of a potential new home to see if downsizing makes financial sense. Sometimes it does not. Depending on property taxes in your area, downsizing to a smaller but newer home may actually result in higher property taxes than you are paying now.

▶ Compare the cost of maintenance between your current home and a potential new one. Things like landscaping, cleaning, and pool maintenance can really add up. Does moving help lower any of those costs? I was amazed at how much time and money we saved by downsizing.

Find Free Hours in Your Week

Time might be the biggest factor keeping you from retirement security. Let's visualize your time each week to identify how many hours you have for picking up additional work to generate more income or for simply sitting down to plan your retirement.

Fill in the calendar on the next page with your weekly obligations. The hour blocks help you clearly see which parts of your day are free. Start by marking off the hours already spoken for in your week, including sleeping, working, and commuting. How many free hours do you have left each day to dedicate to retirement readiness?

Weekly Schedule

	SUN	MON	TUES
6:00 A.M.			
7:00 A.M.			
8:00 A.M.			
9:00 A.M.			
10:00 A.M.			
11:00 A.M.			
12:00 P.M.			
1:00 P.M.			
2:00 P.M.			
3:00 P.M.			
4:00 P.M.			
5:00 P.M.			
6:00 P.M.			
7:00 P.M.			
8:00 P.M.			
9:00 P.M.			
10:00 P.M.			
11:00 P.M.			

WED	THURS	FRI	SAT

Here are some key points to consider when determining how much free time you have:

- Determine whether your time commitments are fixed or flexible. Work is fixed; working out is flexible.

- Be realistic about time frames. Consider travel time and other potential schedule killers.

- Establish a routine for a consistent and predictable schedule.

- Group your tasks together to save time. For example, when I go to the grocery store, I also pick up the dry cleaning.

- Download a time management mobile app to keep you on track.

How many additional hours can you come up with on a weekly basis to supplement your current retirement funds or plans?

Get Creative with Lucrative Hobbies

Now you know how much time you have to dedicate to earning supplemental retirement income, so how should you go about earning it?

There are many additional work opportunities ("side hustles") that are both part-time and fun. Here are some examples of lucrative hobbies to help boost that nest egg:

Boat Tour Guide: People enjoy being on the water, and eco tours are popular now. If you have a boat, consider offering boat tours. Sunset cruises are especially popular with visitors. You could provide a romantic sunset cruise with wine and cheese options for upward of $75 per person.

Crafter: There are so many options in this category, only your imagination will limit you. Sewing, pottery, art, knitting, and quilting are just a few. Not only could you give classes at your local community center or online, you could also sell your arts and crafts at fairs and online on websites like Etsy.

Fishing Guide: People love to know where the best fishing spots are when on vacation and often look for someone to show them. My husband and I often hire a guide for fly fishing when we travel, even though it can be pricey. We have paid up to $300 for a couple of hours on the water. As a guide, not only will you earn extra money but you'll also get someone else to pay for your fishing habit!

Personal Shopper/Driver: Whether picking up groceries or taking people to the airport, personal assistant work can be a great way to earn additional cash on your terms. There are many app-based services you can join to become a driver (such as Uber or Lyft) or do short-term tasks and services (such as Shipt or TaskRabbit). You could place ads in Facebook groups where people are looking for recommendations for local help.

Sports Coach: Golf, tennis, swimming, baseball, and pickleball are common sports in which people look to gain an additional edge. You could offer private lessons or get a part-time job at a club where you could also get a reduction in fees for your own play time.

Flipper: Many people make a lucrative living buying low and selling high. They will scour garage sales and thrift shops looking for marked-down items to sell on eBay, Amazon, or Facebook Marketplace.

Tour Guide: Websites like ToursByLocals allow you to offer your services as a tour guide, many earning $50 an hour on average. If you are passionate about the area you live in and enjoy telling people about the ins and outs of your city, this gig is great, especially if you live in an area with a decent number of tourists. I have a friend in Philadelphia who offers historical tours on the weekends, allowing her to meet new people and get a lot of exercise.

Get creative and be open minded. If you are an empty nester or have independent kids at home, you have more time than you think to start a side business that can bring in extra cash.

Invest the Extra

As you near retirement, begin looking at your money differently. You may not think you have any "extra" funds in your budget, but if you rearrange some assets, you'll find opportunities to grow your nest egg that weren't necessarily available to you in your younger years.

Here are some quick tips:

- Open a traditional IRA if you do not have one, because these types of IRA contributions are tax deductible.

- Contribute the maximum amount if your employer offers 401(k) matching.

- Invest excess savings, like CDs or regular savings accounts, in investment vehicles that will bring a higher interest rate if you already have a year's worth of personal savings set aside for emergencies. Speak with a financial advisor to compare tax advantages and rates of return on annuities and stocks that match your risk tolerance.

- Take advantage of catch-up contributions to your 401(k) and existing IRA accounts.

If you are over 50, you are eligible to make catch-up contributions to your IRA or 401(k). These additional contributions go above the yearly maximums set by the IRS. In 2020, for example, the annual contribution limit for IRAs was $6,000, but catch-up contributions allowed an additional $1,000 investment. For 401(k)s, you could contribute in

2020 up to $6,500 more than the $19,500 annual limit. The several thousand extra these plans allow you to contribute in pre-tax dollars can simultaneously lower your tax bill and boost your retirement accounts. Check with your advisor or contact the IRS to find out current limits.

Adjust Your Spending Habits

The other way to produce extra savings is to reevaluate your budget, especially your spending habits. Reducing your regular expenses can potentially add funds to an IRA or 401(k). This table lists some budget killers for those approaching retirement and suggests actions to mitigate them.

EXPENSE	SAVINGS OPTION
Large family car or SUV no longer necessary	Trade in the vehicle for a less expensive, more fuel-efficient one.
Restaurants and entertainment expenses	Look for alternative free or low-cost entertainment, like downtown Friday Festivals or other community events.
Debt payments with high interest rates	Refinance for lower interest rates, or prioritize making additional payments to reduce your principal.
Home services like lawn care, cleaning services, and pool maintenance	Cancel the services and do them yourself.
Costly health insurance	Shop for a new health insurance plan.*
Mortgage for a large house	Using a website like Airbnb, rent out empty bedrooms left behind by adult children.

*Changes to the Affordable Care Act may allow you to purchase a private health insurance plan for less money than the plans on the marketplace. Also, investigate medical sharing plans, which are health expense cooperatives whose members collectively pay one another's health expenses. I have seen many folks cut their insurance costs by 50 percent or more by joining these programs.

It is always a good idea to look at your budget regardless of your financial situation, and if you are working to increase your retirement savings, start now.

Decide When to Start Taking Social Security Benefits

Social security payments are dramatically different depending on the age at which you choose to retire. You can retire at age 62 and start collecting social security, but waiting to collect until you are 65, 66, or even 67 can increase that payment significantly. This decision is highly personal and based on your circumstances.

Here are some questions to help you decide when to begin taking benefits:

◆ What are your cash needs? Do you have sufficient resources, like investments and other passive income, that will cover your monthly expenses until you request your benefits? If you are struggling to make ends meet and don't foresee adding an income stream in retirement, you may consider taking benefits early.

◆ How long do you estimate your retirement will be? Are you in good health? Do you think you will beat the average life expectancy? If you are not in good health, taking benefits earlier may be the better option.

◆ Do you still want to work part time? If not, earlier benefits might be necessary for you to support yourself.

The Social Security website allows you to sign up for an account that will give you a calculator to determine your social security payments. This tool will help you evaluate your situation to determine whether you should take early payments at age 62 or wait until you are older.

Evaluate Your Pension

If you have a pension, or defined benefit plan, be sure you know what your expected monthly income will be. Typically, a defined benefit plan pays out in two ways: a lump sum or an annuity payment plan with a monthly amount throughout your retirement.

Here are some important questions to cover with your pension plan manager and a financial advisor:

Is the annuity a single life annuity or a joint survivor annuity?
Single life annuities will pay more in total, but they stop paying once you are deceased. If you have a spouse, a joint survivor annuity will continue paying for them.

What are the differences in monthly benefits for the two options?
Do you need the additional income from a single life annuity, or can you make your budget work with the joint survivor plan so the payments will continue for your spouse after your death? Will your spouse be able to maintain their lifestyle once you have passed?

Does the annuity have a fixed rate?
A fixed rate annuity will pay a stable income regardless of how the markets are performing.

Does the annuity offer inflation protection?
Many annuities offer cost of living protections.

What percentage of the annuity can you receive with a lump sum payout?
This amount can range depending on plan rules. More important, keep in mind that you will be responsible for the taxes due on any lump sum you take.

Here are some key points to consider about pensions:

If you take a lump sum from your pension, reinvest it into another retirement vehicle, such as an annuity.
Doing so will help you avoid income tax on the lump sum (which you would have to pay if you were to simply put the money into a savings account), and you will also achieve a higher rate of return than you could with even a high-yield savings account.

If you reinvest the lump sum, determine what amount to take from it regularly as income.
Discuss your options with a financial advisor to understand the income and tax consequences of taking a lump sum.

If your pension is not guaranteed or insured, and there is a risk of your company going bankrupt, taking the lump sum may be the best option for you.
On the other hand, taking a lump sum means no lifetime income.

If you're married, consider whether a single life annuity for a steady monthly income while you're retired is best.
Purchasing a whole life policy to support your spouse upon your death is another consideration.

Your financial needs in retirement are fluid and will evolve over the years. Monitor and rebalance your investment portfolios on a regular basis to keep your goals in line. The closer you get to retirement, the more conservative you should be with your investment strategy. See "Protecting Against Worst-Case Scenarios" pages 81 to 83.

Determine Your Travel Plans

Travel may be on your bucket list for when you retire, and for good reason. You will have the time you need to visit family and old friends and to explore places at your leisure. Now that you have an idea of what your annual budget will be during retirement, you can calculate your annual expendable income, or the amount of money available to you on a yearly basis for travel or other leisure activities after your basic expenses have been paid.

As an example, if you are making $50,000 per year and your expenses in retirement are only $35,000 per year, you will have $15,000 per year to spend on other activities and hobbies. You can determine how much you want of the $15,000 to go toward your travel budget.

To start organizing your plans, make a list of the places you'd like to go:

1. _____

2. _____

3. _____

4. _____

5. _____

6. _____

7. _____

8. _____

9. _____

10. _____

Start researching online the cost of each trip with an eye toward understanding your daily expenses in each place, which include more than just lodging and food. Things like taxis or ride shares, excursions, entrance fees, and even the time of year you travel can impact the overall cost of the trip and are often forgotten in the early planning stages. As an example, going to New York City during the Christmas holiday will be much more expensive than waiting until January to make your trip.

Other travel expenses may crop up when you retire. Consider, for example, weddings, graduations, and other family events you will want to attend. Can you stay with family, or will you need a hotel? Will gifts be required? Will you need to purchase appropriate clothing for your trip?

Here are some potential expenses to bear in mind:

- Airport parking fees
- Airport/plane food and drinks
- ATM fees
- Baggage fees
- Credit card conversion fees
- Currency exchange fees
- Departure tax in foreign countries
- Hotel minibar costs
- Hotel parking costs
- Laundry services
- Pet sitting costs
- Rental car/rental car insurance
- Reservation changes and cancellation fees
- Resort fees
- Room service
- Taxi, ferry, ride share, and ground transfer costs
- Travel insurance
- Wi-Fi charges

Seek Expert Advice

As you approach retirement, look to financial experts to help you evaluate where you are today and where you will be in five or even ten years. Some of the professionals I met with initially were my investment advisors, realtors, CPA, and estate attorney. Here's a checklist of people to contact and what you can expect to learn from each:

☐ **Attorney:** You'll need a lawyer to set up living trusts, wills, or health directives, all of which can affect your retirement. Questions to ask your attorney:

  ▸ Is a will enough?

  ▸ What are the differences between irrevocable and revocable trusts?

  ▸ If I do not have anyone to help with a health directive, whom should I trust?

  ▸ How should I structure my estate and income to protect them from creditors?

☐ **CPA:** If you implement the right tax strategies ahead of time, you can minimize the tax burdens incurred when selling your assets (e.g., a house if you decide to downsize), so keep your accountant updated on your retirement plans. Questions to ask your tax professional every time you meet:

  ▸ Have I taken advantage of all the available tax deductions?

  ▸ Which type of IRA is appropriate at this stage? Self-employment IRA (SEP), traditional, or Roth?

  ▸ What are some ways I can lower my tax bill?

If you are self-employed, also ask your CPA how to create a corporate retirement program as well as the best way to sell your business, if applicable. Is there a way to restructure the business to lessen the tax burden once it's sold?

☐ **Financial advisor:** This person can help you understand what you need to retire, as well as what your potential earnings will be in retirement. They will be able to advise you on how to get the most out of your savings, both now and later. Bring all of your financial information to this meeting, including the budget sheet you filled out earlier this chapter (see page 6). Be prepared to ask the following questions:

  ▸ Will I be able to stay in my current living situation?

  ▸ What is the soonest I will be able to retire if I do nothing?

  ▸ If I need to postpone my retirement, how much longer will I need to work?

  ▸ Should I move to an area with a lower cost of living?

  ▸ Will a side hustle help?

  ▸ What types of IRAs are best for my current situation?

  ▸ What annuities would benefit my situation?

  ▸ Should I change my investment strategy to earn more for my retirement?

  ▸ If I do not have enough for retirement, how do I leave my heirs an inheritance?

☐ **Realtor:** If you own a home or any real estate, many realtors offer a free evaluation of your real estate holdings in an effort to get you to list with them. They can give you a professional opinion on what the market will bring if you decide to sell now or wait two, five, or ten years. Ask the following questions:

- ▸ Where is the market going?

- ▸ Would it be better to wait on selling for a couple of years to capitalize on a hot market?

- ▸ Should I sell now to reduce expenses?

I Have What I Need, Now What Do I Do?

If, after thoroughly vetting your plans and consulting experts for their advice, you find that you have what you need financially for your retirement, congratulations! The next thing you should do is create a plan to ensure you will not outlive your money once you retire. I have seen some retirees get a little overzealous when they retire, purchasing boats, Jet Skis, or other recreational items that take a big chunk out of their retirement savings. Let's go over some steps to make sure your retirement funds stretch without thinning.

Plan Outside Your Retirement Budget

When you established your common retirement expenses in the budget sheet at the beginning of this chapter, you considered recurring costs like insurance premiums, property taxes, utilities, healthcare, housing, and even that annual dream trip (see page 23). But what about those one-time expenses that can take a bite out of your savings? I already warned about keeping large purchases in check, but you may also want to consider other familial needs in early retirement.

Here are some budget killers that can affect your long-term plans:

- College tuition for children or grandchildren

- End-of-life insurance and planning

- Health insurance for your dependents once you leave your job

- Helping your children purchase a home

- Long-term care insurance

- Vacation home purchase

- Weddings

If any of the above apply to you, consider how you will incorporate them into your budget. Can you spread out payments so they don't make a dent in your savings?

Do You Need to Revise Your Budget?

Like all parts of retirement, your budget is not fixed. With age, many expenses go down. Expensive travel may not be a priority in your later years, for example, and may be replaced by time with family and local friends. Children become more independent and no longer need as much assistance. You won't be paying for health insurance or other expenses for family members.

However, in these later stages of retirement, your own health care expenses will start to increase as your health naturally declines. You may experience hospital stays at this point or need in-home care.

Refer to your budget regularly and reassess your expenses for retirement. Are there any changes you need to make now or in the near future?

Redefining Retirement

When you are financially prepared for retirement, you will have the freedom to pursue a full leisure lifestyle, if you wish. But you also may choose to go back to work to fulfill a particular emotional need you may not have realized would crop up in retirement.

Consider a 2014 study by Merrill Lynch and Age Wave, which found that 47 percent of retirees either had worked or planned to work during their retirement, whereas 72 percent of pre-retirees over 50 said they wanted to keep working in some capacity after they retired. Work doesn't just mean a part-time job, either. It could mean volunteering regularly or starting your own business.

Imagine your retirement according to each of the following categories and write down what you picture. What types of activities will you do in each? What feelings do they elicit (joy, fulfillment, accomplishment, etc.)? Try to find something for each category even if you think it will not apply.

Full Leisure

▶ _____

▶ _____

▶ _____

Part-Time Work

▶ _____

▶ _____

▶ _____

Entrepreneurship

- ▸ _____
- ▸ _____
- ▸ _____

Volunteering

- ▸ _____
- ▸ _____
- ▸ _____

Which of these options is most appealing to you? Don't worry about whether it seems realistic right now. When you are trying to define your retirement, you should explore new ideas that bring excitement, even if they don't necessarily seem feasible currently. Ask yourself what changes you can make to get closer to those goals. They may not be that far out of reach once you investigate further.

CHAPTER 2

Finding What Fulfills You

During the honeymoon phase of your retirement, you will love having tons of freedom and experiencing life's pleasures. But many retirees eventually realize that the fun stuff can last only so long. Although joy is an important part of retirement, focusing on leisure can lead to restlessness and a loss of personal value. Eventually, you will want to seek out a more meaningful purpose for your time. The exercises that follow will help you identify what that purpose is.

The Five Stages of Retirement

According to most retirement experts, many retirees will progress through several psychological stages, not unlike the progression through the stages of grief. One such stage includes experiencing a loss of joy. Preparing for what may come allows for a plan that can be put in place before entering a less comfortable phase and can help smooth transitions through retirement.

Stage 1: Pre-Retirement Planning

Planning for retirement can begin as early as your 40s, but most people will start in their 50s or even early 60s. During this stage, your imagination may take over and lead you to dream of all you can do in retirement. You may begin to make lists of everything you want to do.

Stage 2: Anticipation and Excitement

At this point you are counting the days. No more bosses, schedules, or deadlines. You will have complete freedom to do anything you want (or nothing at all!). The prospect of not having to work might even make you giddy.

Stage 3: The Honeymoon

This stage happens during the first few months of retirement. You have a sparkle in your eye, a bounce in your step, and a smile on your face. You are living life on your terms and loving it.

Stage 4: Disenchantment

Reality hits in this stage. There are only so many hobbies you can try, and you may already have lost interest in your original pursuits. You may become disillusioned with retirement and start to question your value. You may even realize your life had more purpose and socialization when you were working. The feelings associated with this stage are why it's so important to have options that bring meaning to your life, such as learning something new, volunteering, or starting a different career.

Stage 5: Stabilization

This stage is where you discover that a happy retirement means finding balance between having fun and having purpose. At this point, look back at your retirement plan and introduce some of the ideas you had during the planning stages that bring balance back to your retirement.

EXERCISE 1: List Your 10 Retirement Commandments

In this exercise, we are going to create your 10 Retirement Commandments—the precepts you would like to follow to ensure your retirement serves your fundamental goals. Consider which aspects of your life you are not willing to compromise on during your retirement. It may be as simple as committing to helping others, or as difficult as letting go of old grudges. One of my favorite personal commandments is, "Don't miss out on something great because it is difficult or scary."

Your commandments may have to do with healthy habits or a boundary you set for yourself, such as staying out of debt. Whatever your commandments are, be sure to keep the list concise and attainable. If ever you find yourself disenchanted with retirement, come back to this list.

One of the keys to happiness in retirement is being flexible. The ideas you have now may not work out the way you thought, so you may need to alter this list as you progress through your retirement, based on your shifting needs and desires. Surrendering to the ever-changing process is important to maintaining your joy.

Rachel, 68
Former Paralegal, Leesburg, Florida

"As I got closer to retirement, my 10 commandments changed all the time. They went from being self-serving to serving others. It was then that I began to live to my full potential!"

1. _____

_____

2. _____

_____

3. _____

_____

4. _____

_____

5. _____

_____

6. _____

_____

7. _____

_____

8. _____

_____

9. _____

_____

10. _____

_____

Exercise 2: **Identify Your Values**

Along with your personal commandments, your long-term retirement goals should be based on your core values. These beliefs are what is important to you and you alone—no outside influence from friends or family. Assessing your values without input from others will give you a strong sense of self.

Circle the values below that are most important in helping you understand your priorities.

Family   Spirituality   Volunteering   Fitness

Equality   Environmentalism   Travel   Continuous learning

Financial stability   The arts   Nature   Healthy eating

Giving   Political activism   Ancestry   Diversity

Justice   World peace   Mental health   Friendship

Top Three Values and Related Activities

Once you have circled your values, list your top three in order of importance, number one being the most important. Write down some activities that relate to your top three values that can help you live out those values during your retirement.

If one of your core values is volunteering, you might be interested in joining the Peace Corps for a two-year commitment overseas. Or, if family is high on your list, you may want to commit to babysitting your grandchildren once a month or having lunch with a sibling once a week.

1. Value: _____

    a. Activity 1: _____

    b. Activity 2: _____

    c. Activity 3: _____

2. Value: _____

    a. Activity 1: _____

    b. Activity 2: _____

    c. Activity 3: _____

3. Value: _____

    a. Activity 1: _____

    b. Activity 2: _____

    c. Activity 3: _____

EXERCISE 3: **Find Your Hobbies**

Hobbies are different from your values in that hobbies primarily serve to spark joy and provide a chance to do something just for your own enjoyment. Hobbies can be very fulfilling during retirement—emotionally, physically, and intellectually.

Circle your top three current hobbies. Next, place a check mark next to those you would like to try. Finally, draw a dollar sign ($) next to hobbies you can potentially monetize. Thinking through different aspects of your hobbies will help you identify new areas to enrich your retirement, whether for additional income or for pleasure.

Acting or community theater	Antiquing	Archery	Art collecting	Astronomy
Auto restoration	Baking	Ballet	Ballroom dancing	Baseball
Basketball	Beekeeping	Biking	Billiards	Bingo
Bird watching	Blogging	Board games	Boating	Bonsai gardening
Book club	Book collecting	Botany	Bowling	Bridge
Calligraphy	Camping	Canning	Canoeing	Cheese making
Chess	Classic cars	Coaching	Coin collecting	Coloring
Composting	Computer coding	Cooking	Craft cocktails	Crafting
Crafting parties	Creative writing	Crocheting	Cycling	Deep sea fishing
Dinner parties	Drawing	Embroidery	Event-watching parties (like the Oscars or Olympics)	Fashion

Fishing	Foreign language	Furniture restoration	Gardening	Genealogy
Geocaching	Glass blowing	Going to a gym	Golf	Guns/gun range
Ham radio	Hiking	Historian	Homebrewing	Horseback riding
Hunting	Hydroponics	Interior design	Jewelry making	Kayaking
Kite sailing	Knitting	Learning a new language online	Learning an instrument	Library volunteer
Line dancing	Metal detecting	Meteorology	Military organization clubs	Mini-golf
Model building	Movie collecting	Music collecting	Origami	Painting
Participate in online forums	Pet care	Photography	Pickleball	Playing music
Podcasting	Poetry	Pottery	Quilting	Race car driving
Racquetball	Rotary clubs	Running/ jogging	RV'ing	School alumni clubs
Scrapbooking	Scuba diving	Sculpture	Sewing	Shell collecting
Shopping	Singing	Skeet shooting	Skiing	Snorkeling
Softball	Spoken word poetry	Sport memorabilia collecting	Stained glass	Stamp collecting
Stand-up paddle board	Surf fishing	Surfing	Swimming	Swing dancing
Table tennis	Teaching	Team sports	Tennis	Thrifting
Touch football	Trains	TV memorabilia	Video games	Walking
Watercolor art	Welding	Wine collecting	Wood working	Yoga

Social media is a great way to find groups of like-minded people who do hobbies or activities together. For example, local foodies have meet-ups to try new restaurants or tasting menus. This activity could even become a small side business where you sell tickets to the event. Restaurants usually offer a discount on a set menu for a group.

Track Your Hobby-Related Expenses

For potential new hobbies, research what is involved in getting started, and look online for related clubs or groups in your area. Make sure you research the potential financial impact as well, such as the cost of equipment or hobby-related travel.

Make a shopping list below for the top three hobbies you want to try during retirement and how much those hobbies cost. You can even start purchasing these hobby-related items while you are still working so they have less of an impact on your retirement budget.

Hobby _____

1. Item _____ $ _____

2. Item: _____ $ _____

3. Item: _____ $ _____

4. Item: _____ $ _____

5. Item: _____ $ _____

Total Cost: $ _____

Hobby _____

1. Item: _____ $ _____

2. Item: _____ $ _____

3. Item: _____ $ _____

4. Item: _____ $ _____

5. Item: _____ $ _____

Total Cost: $ _____

Hobby _____

1. Item: _____ $ _____

2. Item: _____ $ _____

3. Item: _____ $ _____

4. Item: _____ $ _____

5. Item: _____ $ _____

Total Cost: $ _____

EXERCISE 4: **Make a Difference**

Giving back to your community to help others with information or assistance based on your experience and acquired wisdom is a great way to find purpose during retirement because doing so betters the lives of others. Many people and organizations can benefit from your offerings.

Think back to your values. Were any of them related to social or political change? Think about the things that keep you up at night on a local, national, or global level: Are you concerned for the economy or the environment? Do you have concerns about the political landscape or social injustice? What about animal rights? These areas are where you might have an impact and can consider seeking volunteer opportunities.

Volunteer Areas

Write down the top five issues you'd like to volunteer with, in order of importance.

1. _____

2. _____

3. _____

4. _____

5. _____

What are your skills and knowledge based in? Make a list of your top 10 skills and strengths. Some examples could be entrepreneurship, financial literacy, teaching, managing, or staging a retail store.

1. _____

2. _____

3. _____

4. _____

5. _____

6. _____

7. _____

8. _____

9. _____

10. _____

Once you have assessed your skills, look for a common theme. Which issues related to your top values require the types of skills you can provide?

EXERCISE 5: **Look for Places to Give Back**

Do an internet search of local charities that align with your interests and skills. Most organizations have a volunteer coordinator who will assess your skills and offer a list of events to participate in. Consider these example organizations and institutions:

Children's safe homes: Provide tutoring, clothing, and financial literacy.

Habitat for Humanity: Help with a variety of tasks from building homes to sorting through donations for this organization, which provides access to low-income home ownership and financial education.

Homeless shelters: Help provide job skill training, job placement, tutoring, or career counseling. More than just temporary housing, these facilities offer a variety of resources and are typically grouped by gender or family. You can choose men's, women's, or family shelters.

Hospitals: Volunteer to pass out books, magazines, and meals, and help visitors.

Libraries: Organize and file books and assist in other tasks, including fundraising.

Local sports and recreation leagues: Offer coaching and mentoring in sports.

Pet shelters: Walk, play with, foster, or train animals.

SafeSpace: Donate clothing and toys, especially around the holidays, to this women's shelter.

Schools: Tutor students in school subjects or financial and language literacy, or purchase school supplies for students in need.

SCORE: Assist with paperwork or other tasks for entrepreneurs or small-business owners who want to start or expand a business.

After researching each organization, write down the areas where you feel you can give back the most. As an example, Habitat for Humanity offers volunteering opportunities in both its construction and ReStore (reuse store) divisions. Within those two categories, there are several areas where you can be of assistance, such as merchandise display in the ReStore or volunteering on the construction sites one day per week for three months of service.

Where to Volunteer

List the organizations you are most interested in volunteering with, the top three areas within those organizations that match the skills you listed in exercise 4 (see page 44), and the contact information for each area of the organization.

Organization: _____

Areas of Interest

1. _____

    Contact Name: _____

    Contact Phone: _____

    Contact Email: _____

2. _____

    Contact Name: _____

    Contact Phone: _____

    Contact Email: _____

3. _____

   Contact Name: _____

   Contact Phone: _____

   Contact Email: _____

Organization: _____

Areas of Interest

1. _____

   Contact Name: _____

   Contact Phone: _____

   Contact Email: _____

2. _____

   Contact Name: _____

   Contact Phone: _____

   Contact Email: _____

3. _____

   Contact Name: _____

   Contact Phone: _____Contact

   Email: _____

Organization: _____

Areas of Interest

1. _____

    Contact Name: _____

    Contact Phone: _____

    Contact Email: _____

2. _____

    Contact Name: _____

    Contact Phone: _____

    Contact Email: _____

3. _____

    Contact Name: _____

    Contact Phone: _____

    Contact Email: _____

Be on the lookout for paid opportunities as well. Many organizations offer part-time positions that can give you additional income. Be careful not to overcommit your time, though. You will want to maintain balance during retirement.

EXERCISE 6: **Prioritize Spirituality**

For many, spirituality is as important as charity work or exploring a passion. This exercise will help you recognize where you are on your spiritual walk and determine how much time and energy you would like to dedicate to it in retirement.

1. Do you have a regular spiritual practice? If not, are you interested in beginning one? Write about it here.

   _____

2. Are you currently a member of a spiritual or religious organization? Circle: Y / N

3. If yes, are you involved with any groups or activities in this organization? Write them here, or list any you would like to learn more about.

   _____

4. Do you feel you are making progress in your spiritual journey? Answer here, describing why or why not.

   _____

Spiritual Habits

Do you have any of the following habits in your spiritual life? If so, rate their importance on a scale from 1 to 10, with 10 being the highest level of importance. Then assess how much time you dedicate to these practices every week.

SPIRITUAL PRACTICE	IMPORTANCE (1-10)	HOURS DEDICATED WEEKLY
Fasting	_____	_____
Fellowship	_____	_____
Journaling	_____	_____
Meditation	_____	_____
Prayer	_____	_____
Stewardship	_____	_____
Other	_____	_____

Are you happy with this level of commitment? How much more time, if any, are you willing to add to this part of your life? Consider which practices you might like to commit more to.

EXERCISE 7: **Putting It All Together**

With a better understanding of your values, hobbies, skills, and passions, decide how much time you want to commit to them.

Consider my retirement schedule: I have a weekly dinner with my family on Wednesdays from 6 to 8 p.m. I go to the gym Sundays through Wednesdays in the midafternoon. We also have a fellowship meeting with people from our congregation on Saturday mornings from 10:30 a.m. to 1:00 p.m. Fridays are completely booked: I go to the chiropractor, have lunch with the girls, and do my grocery shopping, then I go home and finish my cleaning for the weekend. For any activities like the ones I just mentioned, you will want to cross off these times as "busy." Doing so will show you what time you have available to commit to volunteering and hobbies.

On the next page is a sample calendar with my weekly activities filled in. I can now see that I have most mornings and all day Thursday and Saturday available for volunteering.

You already filled out a calendar in chapter 1 with your current schedule (see page 14)—now it's time to envision your weekly routine during retirement. Use the calendar on pages 54 and 55 to write down any of your daily or weekly commitments, such as church meetings, sports leagues, healthcare, or family obligations you already know you will have in retirement. Do not include time spent working unless you will be continuing that work into retirement.

Weekly Schedule

	SUN	MON	TUES	WED	THURS	FRI	SAT
6:00 AM							
7:00 AM							
8:00 AM						Chiropractor	
9:00 AM							
10:00 AM							
11:00 AM							Fellowship Meeting
12:00 PM						Lunch	
1:00 PM							
2:00 PM						Groceries	
3:00 PM	Gym	Gym	Gym	Gym			
4:00 PM							
5:00 PM						Clean House	
6:00 PM							
7:00 PM				Family Dinner			
8:00 PM							
9:00 PM							
10:00 PM							

Weekly Schedule

	SUN	MON	TUES
6:00 A.M.			
7:00 A.M.			
8:00 A.M.			
9:00 A.M.			
10:00 A.M.			
11:00 A.M.			
12:00 P.M.			
1:00 P.M.			
2:00 P.M.			
3:00 P.M.			
4:00 P.M.			
5:00 P.M.			
6:00 P.M.			
7:00 P.M.			
8:00 P.M.			
9:00 P.M.			
10:00 P.M.			
11:00 P.M.			

WED	THURS	FRI	SAT

Scheduling out your time in this way will also make clear how much time you are dedicating to purposeful activities versus fun or leisure. You might find that this balance is leisure heavy at the beginning of your retirement, but to find purpose and validation in retirement, strike a balance between fun and valuable activities that bring you fulfillment.

Here are some key points to keep in mind:

- Don't overcommit. Leave free time so you can be flexible if other events or activities come up that you are interested in.

- Don't be afraid to say no if something does not work with your schedule.

- Don't allow friends and family to influence the process if you do not want them to. These reflections are about finding *your* purpose.

- Be open to trying new things! Retirement offers the opportunity to experience new activities you might not have had time for previously.

Is filling out a calendar of your future schedule too specific for your current stage of retirement planning? Maybe you need to zoom out and simply consider what types of activities a great week in retirement might include. Use this chart to imagine what your best week in retirement would be versus your worst week.

BEST WEEK ACTIVITIES	WORST WEEK ACTIVITIES

Use this chart as a guide to narrow your focus, then return to the calendar when you have a better idea of how your "best week" activities will fit into your weekly retirement schedule.

CHAPTER 3

Dreaming Big

In this chapter, we are going to do some dream build-ing, which means thinking BIG. Prepare to use your imagination and dig deep as you explore your personal aspirations in retirement.

The Future Is Bright

As of 2017, the Centers for Disease Control and Prevention reported the average life expectancy in the United States to be 78 years old. If you are a woman, you can expect to live into your eighties. And our life expectancy continues to rise as medical technology evolves. That means plenty of life to be lived once you retire.

My retirement goal is to try things I was hesitant about when I was younger, either because I had children in tow or because I was just plain fearful. For example, I am scared of heights, so last year I made sure to try zip lining. I was terrified, but I was equally as committed to pushing my limits while still physically able. So far, I have learned fly fishing, hiked to the top of a mountain, and conquered white water rafting.

Your goals might be completely different. Skydiving may not be on your list, but maybe you have always wanted to teach an art class or own a retail shop in that cool mountain town where you spent summers with your family. In 2017, the financial services company Aegon did a Retirement Readiness Survey asking for people's number one retirement aspiration. Here's what respondents said:

Aspirations

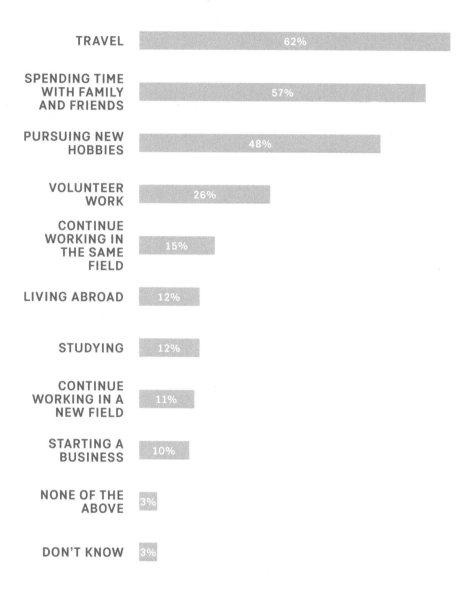

TRAVEL	62%
SPENDING TIME WITH FAMILY AND FRIENDS	57%
PURSUING NEW HOBBIES	48%
VOLUNTEER WORK	26%
CONTINUE WORKING IN THE SAME FIELD	15%
LIVING ABROAD	12%
STUDYING	12%
CONTINUE WORKING IN A NEW FIELD	11%
STARTING A BUSINESS	10%
NONE OF THE ABOVE	3%
DON'T KNOW	3%

Consider the above options as you explore your retirement aspirations. Whatever you decide, make sure you are following *your* personal goals and not allowing your friends and family to influence you too much at this stage.

EXERCISE 1: **Rank Your Aspirations**

Taking the general aspirations from the survey, number them in order of importance in your life, with 1 being the most important and 10 being the least. Think about what each aspiration looks like in your life and answer the questions. Put an X next to any aspirations you have no interest in pursuing.

___Traveling

Where do you want to go? How do you plan on getting there? _____

___Spending time with family and friends

Will you be traveling to see family or planning events?

_____

___Pursuing new hobbies

What new hobbies interested you on the list you created in exercise 3 of chapter 2 (see page 40)? _____

_____

___Volunteer work

List the places you are interested in volunteering or the types of volunteer work that suit your skills. _____

_____

___Continue working in the same field

Will you stay with the same company in a part-time capacity or eventually transition to a new position?

_____

___Living abroad

Which countries are you interested in living in? Why?

_____

___Studying

What degrees or skills are you interested in obtaining?

_____

___Continue working in a new field

What new career are you interested in pursuing?

_____

___Starting a business

What type of business have you considered? What business suits your skills and knowledge base? _____

_____

From Dream to Reality

Now that you have assessed your aspirations, answer these questions to start making them a reality:

What are your top three aspirations in retirement?

1. _____

2. _____

3. _____

What are three things you must do or accomplish within each of your top three aspirations?

Aspiration: _____

1. _____

2. _____

3. _____

Aspiration: _____

1. _____

2. _____

3. _____

Aspiration: _____

1. _____

2. _____

3. _____

EXERCISE 2: **Consider Your Living Situation**

Many people aspire to relocate to a new area when they retire, possibly because their children have moved away or they are craving a warmer climate or need a lower cost of living. You might also be looking to downsize or even live abroad. According to *Forbes*, 85 percent of people who move to another country are happier than they were in their previous home, so becoming an expat is an option many people consider during the pre-retirement planning stage.

Let's look at some ways to decide where you will live during retirement.

Downsizing: If downsizing but staying in your current city is the direction for you, you will want to check out smaller homes in neighborhoods where you'd like to live. Venture out and look at some open houses. Visit some retirement communities and get brochures on what they have to offer. Start to imagine yourself living in a different home. Do you want a home that is maintenance free or offers activities for the 55-and-up community?

Moving away: If you are planning to leave the city, state, or country in retirement, start planning vacations in the area you're considering. Rent an Airbnb in neighborhoods where you may want to live to get a feel for that area. Find other retirees who have done the same and ask about their experiences. Start to build relationships online so you already know people when you get there.

Staying in your current home: Is your home a viable option to age in place? Do you foresee the repairs, maintenance, and expenses being manageable as you get older? Do you have help available for cleaning and upkeep if you need it?

WHAT RETIREMENT LOOKS LIKE ABROAD

According to NPR, the rest of the world is beginning to retire around the same age as Americans (between 65 and 67), but retirement looks different in various parts of the world. Let's look at a couple of other countries and get a glimpse of what retirement is like for them.

France

In France, retirement used to begin as early as 52 and citizens were required to retire by the age of 67. Due to a law passed in 2008, the French are now permitted to work until 70, but most retire between 65 and 67.

With the number one health care system in the EU, the French government provides shelters for retirees who need assistance with memory care and other elderly issues. They also have a robust pension system, with the average French citizen earning 50 to 55 percent of their income in retirement.

Japan

In Japan, the elderly make up almost 25 percent of the population, and the country has taken the initiative in helping them find purpose in their daily lives through the intergenerational activity program REPRINTS. This program provides a volunteer network, primarily through the school system, whereby retirees can offer their wisdom and talents to younger generations. This work has shown great health benefits for the elderly in Japan.

The Library of Congress projected a shortage of caregivers by 2025 for the 20 million elderly in Japan, prompting the country to create a fleet of "carebots" to help care for the aging population. These bots offer cleaning services as well as assistance with health care needs.

Deciding Where to Relocate

If you are committed to moving, list three places to investigate for your new home. Take into consideration factors such as climate and access to services like hospitals and doctors, activities, and entertainment. Also, investigate the cost of living, distance from family and friends, and population size. Place all these factors in their respective pro or con categories to help you visualize which options have clear advantages.

1. Location: _____

PRO	CON

2. Location: _____

PRO	CON

3. Location: _____

PRO	CON

EXERCISE 3: Ten Things You Must Have to Be Happy in Retirement

Let's look to the future and think about the "must-haves" for your retirement. Some may prioritize traveling regularly or pursuing a hobby full-time. For me, it's being close to my grandchildren and having a second career completely different from the financial services industry. For others, the priority may be living on the road. What are your must-haves to be happy? Try to be specific and actionable—these might be aspirations, but they should still be possible within your abilities and means.

1. _____

2. _____

3. _____

4. _____

5. _____

6. _____

7. _____

8. _____

9. _____

10. _____

Once you have your list of must-haves, refer to exercise 1 in this chapter (see page 62), where you ranked your aspirations. Are there any must-haves on this list you did not write in exercise 1? How do these must-haves compare to your aspirations in terms of importance?

James, 62
Former Attorney, Cleveland, Tennessee

"Life is like a wheel—your faith, family, finances, work, and friends are the spokes of that wheel. When your spokes are uneven, your wheel does not turn very well."

EXERCISE 4: **Five Adventures You Never Thought You'd Be Brave Enough to Take**

Now that we know what you need practically to guide you toward a happy retirement, let's get back to dream building. Retirement is all about exploring new ideas, pushing past fears, and breaking barriers. What better way to tackle these challenges than through adventure? List five adventures you would like to have once you retire that you might not have felt brave enough to pursue previously. Adventures could look like hiking a mountain range, auditioning for a talent competition, or taking a cross-country road trip.

1. _____

2. _____

3. _____

4. _____

5. _____

Now write down three things you can do to make these adventures a reality in retirement. Circle any that overlap with the ways to achieve your aspirations from exercise 1 (see page 62) or your must-haves from exercise 3 (see page 69).

Adventure: _____

1. _____

2. _____

3. _____

Adventure: _____

   1. _____

   2. _____

   3. _____

Adventure: _____

   1. _____

   2. _____

   3. _____

Adventure: _____

   1. _____

   2. _____

   3. _____

Adventure: _____

   1. _____

   2. _____

   3. _____

THOUGHT STARTERS

If you're having trouble coming up with retirement aspirations, must-haves, or adventures, consider any of the following thought starters to spark an idea. Though you should focus on your individual pursuits as a guide to these questions, talking about them with family or friends may be helpful to brainstorm. Just be careful not to let outside influence sway you into any big decisions.

1. What are you grateful for in life?
2. What stretches or challenges you?
3. What were you most passionate about in your career?
4. What about the world would you like to change?
5. When you think about the future, what gets you excited?
6. What life lessons have affected you the most?
7. What was your hardest mistake to learn from?
8. Who do you compare yourself to?
9. When was the last time you tried something new?
10. What do you wish you did more of when you were younger?
11. What do you want to be doing in five or ten years?
12. What would you do differently if you thought no one would judge you?
13. What is your biggest regret in life?
14. What does joy look like to you?
15. What activities cause you to lose track of time?
16. What do you want to accomplish during retirement?
17. When you are 80, what do you want to be able to look back on?
18. Is there anything holding you back?
19. How old do you think you act?
20. What makes you smile?
21. What wrongs do you want to right?
22. If you were to make a time capsule, what would you put in it?
23. What is the one book everyone should read?
24. When was the last time you sat in complete silence, and for how long?
25. What does the retirement dream look like to you?

Part II

Living Your Values

Now that you understand your personal goals for retirement, it's time to consider how they will affect your loved ones. In this part of the book, you will take what you've learned about your financial situation and retirement aspirations and put them into action by creating a plan for the many different paths your retirement might take.

CHAPTER 4
Living Flexibly

At this point, you have a pretty good idea of where you stand both financially and emotionally for your retirement. But where will you be in five years, or ten? Things happen that are beyond your control, and your plans may need to change accordingly. That's why the most important aspect of retirement planning is flexibility.

Aligning with Family Goals

Thus far throughout the book, I have asked you to consider only your own thoughts and feelings when making your retirement plans so you could get a sense of your individual goals and aspirations without outside influence. However, it is likely that you have others to consider when making your retirement plans, so let's talk about aligning your plans with your loved ones' priorities, goals, and values.

There are several scenarios to consider when it comes to retirement plans that include spouses, children, parents, and even extended family. You will want to have open and honest conversations with your family members concerning your wants, desires, and plans. How will your choices affect them? Are they on board with what you want your retirement to look like? Consider the questions below when discussing your goals with your family—they're broken down by whom your retirement may impact.

Spouse

- If you have a younger spouse who still has several years until they reach retirement age, should you delay your retirement until your spouse is ready to retire (and save more money in the process)? What will your lifestyle look like if you are retired and your spouse is still working?

- What does your spouse's idea of retirement look like? How does it differ from yours?

- Does your spouse have outside family obligations that you need to take into consideration? Aging parents and dependent children can affect how you plan your retirement.

Children

- If you have children who are still home or financially dependent on you, making changes to your financial situation may affect them as well. Will you sell your home to support your retirement if there are still children living there?

- What time frames and boundaries have you set with your children when it comes to them becoming financially independent?

Parents or Other Elders

- Do you have any elderly family members you have taken responsibility for? How will caring for them impact your retirement plans (including financial or timeline planning)?

- Are they able to remain where they are currently living, or is there a plan in place for you to care for them?

Other Family

- Do you need to be in close proximity to your extended family to help them? Are they willing to move closer to you, or are you considering moving closer to them?

- If you have siblings who are a part of your retirement conversations, how do they fit into your plans? Do your siblings share your retirement lifestyle goals and values?

Sandra, 69
Former Teacher, The Villages, Florida

"I started my retirement as the main caregiver for my elderly mother and my husband, who had health issues that kept us at home. Learning how to navigate retirement alone was tough, but I found fulfillment in part-time work, local social clubs, and any activities that helped get me out of the house. It was not what I expected to happen, but I was able to find support and purpose within my local community. After I recovered from their passing, I was lucky enough to marry again and am now able to travel and do the things I dreamed about in retirement."

Preparing for Financial Loss

One day in 2010, I stopped at a convenience store to get gas. As I was looking around the parking lot, I saw an old high school friend's dad drive up in his 700 Series BMW. When I approached him to say hello, I noticed he was wearing a security guard uniform. This man had retired years ago from the citrus industry and seemingly had it all. He and his wife lived in a beautiful home on the river that would have easily been worth $800K to $900K before 2008. He told me he had put a lot of his money into a local bank's stocks, but the bank failed during the crisis and all their money was lost. They had put their home on the market, but there were no buyers for the price they believed the home was worth. They were financially ruined, and he'd had to get a job as a security guard to make ends meet.

It was a stark reminder that the economy is always a factor for retirees. While you are working, stock market dips are not too much of a concern because there's time for the markets to recover. We all remember the 2008 recession when the housing market crashed and took the stock market along with it. It took almost 10 years to see a recovery to 2006 housing prices. Even some folks who had pensions saw an adjustment in their income or lost their pensions altogether.

During that time, many folks needed to continue working to wait out the economy's recovery or were forced to sell assets at a time when unemployment was high and housing and stock prices were low. There was an expression I heard a lot during those years: "A lot of millionaires will be made by this recession." But many millionaires would also be unmade.

You just never know when the next disaster, pandemic, or market crash is coming or how long it will last. When the COVID-19 pandemic began in 2020, many believed it would be short lived. The only dependable projection for disasters during retirement is that they will continue to occur. Are you prepared to withstand those darker times?

Protecting Against Worst-Case Scenarios

Here are my top 10 recommendations for disaster-proofing your retirement savings:

1. **Balance your portfolio to protect your assets.** Invest in a diverse portfolio that can withstand different industries taking hits in the market without your whole portfolio crumbling. (In other words, don't put all your eggs in one basket.) The good news is that the markets have always come back and restored the losses they incurred. The key is to be able to wait out those time frames while things recover.

2. **Maintain a healthy cash savings.** In theory, putting all your money in the stock market sounds good because you will earn a higher rate of return than you would from a savings account, but if the market crashes, you'll be left with no safety net. It's smarter to keep one

year's worth of expenses in a savings account in case of market volatility.

3. **Prepare and stick to a budget.** Make sure you annualize your budget so you can compare it to your annual expenses. When you see your expenses on an annual basis, those small (but frequent) purchases can really add up—like spending $1,500 a year on drive-thru coffee.

4. **Learn where you can minimize your monthly bills.** Things like monthly subscriptions for items or services you no longer use but still pay for can drain you financially. A friend recently told me she had been continuing to pay for Audible despite having years of book credits. Cancel those subscriptions!

5. **Pay down your debts and stay out of debt.** Do not let that luxury trip to Italy or pricey recreational toys suck you in if you'll be paying for them (and the interest they come with) over time.

6. **Maintain your assets and keep them in good repair.** If you need to sell your home quickly, you do not want to be in the position of having to make costly last-minute repairs because you've let things go over the years.

7. **Switch to credit cards with lower interest rates.**

8. **Compare insurance rates for your home and auto plans annually** to make sure you're taking advantage of the best price on the market and checking that your coverage is appropriate for what you need. Often people are under- or overinsured.

9. **Set boundaries with adult children** who have had a difficult time becoming financially independent. Having a firm end date of support is often what they need to achieve independence.

10. **Move quickly when you see trouble on the horizon.**
    When COVID-19 hit the United States in March
    2020, my husband and I immediately put ourselves
    on a spending freeze. We had no idea if our real estate
    income would be impacted. Fortunately, all our ten-
    ants were able to pay their rent, but it could have been
    much worse.

Jack, 61
Former Conference Services Manager,
Tampa, Florida

*"Enjoy your retirement, but be relentless in protecting
your retirement funds. Filling your time without spending
money can be a challenge."*

Death of a Spouse

We know it will happen someday, but none of us can plan
exactly which day that will be. Aside from bringing grief, the
death of a spouse during retirement can have many implica-
tions depending on which spouse passes. My husband had a
customer who passed from brain cancer and his wife had no
knowledge of their finances. She was then daunted by the task
of going through mounds of paperwork to figure out where
all the accounts were and what her financial situation was.
Things were in total disarray.

Losing a spouse can also mean a loss of income if you were
dependent on their social security or pension plan. When my
stepmother passed unexpectedly, it was difficult for my father
to maintain his lifestyle. She was the healthier one, so it never
occurred to him he might have to live without her income.

We tend to get stuck in our ideas of what we think will happen versus being open to many different scenarios. Have a plan in place for each spouse if the other should pass suddenly.

Here are some key points to help you and your spouse prepare for each other's unanticipated death.

- **Get organized.** Life insurance policies, annuities, pension plans, social security, and other important financial documents should be readily available to both spouses. Even if one spouse does not want to know any of the details, they should still know exactly how to find the names of health professionals and online usernames and passwords and other such information. Make sure everything is in file folders and labeled correctly so anyone who needs to access your records can find what they're looking for.

- **Make a list of emergency contacts** you keep in your wallet and in your home.

- **Have short-term emergency funds available** to assist the other spouse with at least six months of living expenses.

- **Make sure all your insurance beneficiary information is up to date and accurate.**

- **Add your spouse to your bank accounts as a POD (payable on death).** If you and your spouse maintain separate bank accounts, this designation will give you both access to each other's funds without having the account go through probate court (the legal proceeding for settling debts after death). Probate can hold up those funds for 90 days or longer and place a burden on your loved ones trying to resolve your final expenses.

- **Evaluate your life insurance.** Does your spouse need an extra cushion to make it through their lifetime?

The bottom line is this: Preparing for the death of a spouse makes things easier on those left behind.

Leaving Your Legacy: Estate Planning

Estate planning is one of the most important things you can do to preserve your wealth and create a legacy for your family. It can also be the key to an easy transition for your heirs. Not only can the right plan help you in life, it can also help your survivors in death. As an example, revocable living trusts are a retirement and estate planning vehicle that can help protect you from creditors and Medicare bills. The trust will allow you to pass your estate to your beneficiaries without having them go through probate.

Meet with an attorney to discuss your options for establishing trusts, health care mandates, and wills, as well as how to structure them to benefit your estate and ensure your family has an inheritance. If you've already done your estate planning, you'll want to double-check with an attorney that it is still valid. Did you know when you move across state lines your will may become invalid?

To help that appointment go smoothly, come prepared with information on your insurance, assets, bank accounts, liabilities, and beneficiaries.

John, 69
Former Attorney, Vero Beach, Florida

"Planning out your estate relieves your family members of the burden later, unless of course you want them to suffer!"

Changing Future Plans

There are many reasons your plans may change in retirement. We never know what the future holds or, more important, who will move into or out of our lives. Again, the key is to remain flexible and open to new ideas. Let's look at some scenarios you may encounter in retirement that might change your plans.

My family is moving: I never thought in a million years my daughter would move away, but she wanted her children to go to a particular school. We are very close, and she didn't want to go without us, so we compromised. We agreed to sell one of our properties in Florida and purchase a new home with her, with plans to go between her guest home and Florida. Because we were flexible, we were able to come up with a plan to stay close and not miss a minute with our grandchildren.

My spouse has passed: When my father and stepmother were still alive, my stepmother mentioned that if and when my father passed, she wanted to leave Florida and move back up to her hometown in Ohio. She was okay with living in Florida with him, but she did not want to be alone there. She wanted to be closer to her children if my father was not in the picture. A similar situation may become a reality for you, too, if you lose your spouse and don't want to continue your retirement where you started it.

I want to be closer to friends: Many of my high school friends moved back to our hometown for retirement. They reconnected on social media and have hosted mini-reunions in person. Once you retire, you may realize you miss the socialization of work and want to be closer to old friends.

I no longer like the climate I live in: I have seen many retirees move to a warmer climate even though they swore they never would. As we age, shoveling snow and dealing with frozen water pipes can be less appealing. The cold can also affect our health negatively. If you have the means, one option is to become a snowbird and buy a second home so you can be up north in the summer and south in the winter. Another option might be to rent a house somewhere warm for the winter months.

I met someone new: If you are a solo retiree, you're far from alone. Many other solo retirees are also looking for companionship and romance. A friend of mine met her second husband during retirement and ended up selling everything she owned and moving 50 miles to be with him. Retired life is just as unpredictable as in your working years!

I need to reduce my expenses (over time or all at once): Many retirees realize after they begin retirement that they do not have enough income to maintain their lifestyle. Rising property taxes and insurance costs spur many to move to a more affordable area. States like Arizona, Florida, South Carolina, and Tennessee depend heavily on retirees relocating there and want to make sure they remain an attractive option for those coming from other areas. In Florida, there is a rising movement to put a cap on seniors' property taxes for this reason. Speaking of taxes, metropolitan areas have extremely high property values, but the property taxes are equally tall (as are other taxes, such as state income tax). If a market crash happens on top of those costs, you may have to reconsider where you live.

Jamie, 72
Former Business Owner, Palm Beach
Gardens, Florida

"The best part about retirement is you can change your plans whenever you want!"

CHAPTER 5
Living Free

In the previous chapters, we focused on the big picture. Now it's time to zoom in and take stock of the smaller rituals that will fill up your time during retirement. These differ from the hobbies you listed in exercise 3 of chapter 2 (see page 40) in that they are simpler pleasures, often only moments of time, but they add up over the long term to create a general feeling of happiness. Rituals fill in the spaces between activities in your regular routine, lower stress, and allow you to live in the moment.

Daily Rituals

Earlier, I discussed creating a weekly routine that included things like going to the gym and meeting friends for lunch once a week. These weekly routines help you get out of the house and keep you connected to your loved ones, but what happens in between those activities? That's where rituals come in. I'll list mine here to prompt you to think about any you may want to incorporate in your own life in retirement.

Rituals I Have Added to My Daily Retirement Routine

Since beginning my retirement, I have picked up some habits I look forward to throughout the day because they bring positive predictability and consistent doses of happiness.

Gardening: When I was working, I often tried maintaining a small vegetable garden. Some years I was successful, and others I was not. The minute I left my job, I made sure my gardening beds were ready for the next season because I knew I could commit the time my garden would need. Every day when I take the dog out in the afternoon, I do a little weeding, watering, and inspecting of my plants. Gardening is something I look forward to when I have been on the computer all day. I can get some sun and fresh air while working at creating a food forest in my yard that also provides fresh organic vegetables for a healthy lifestyle. I find gardening extremely fulfilling because of the process of nurturing something from seed to an edible product that contributes to my family.

Stretching: I do have certain days I go to the gym throughout the week, but I also have a daily ritual of stretching and making sure I stay limber. Running my business from home means I only need to leave my couch a few times a day to eat, sleep, and go to the bathroom. I can get engrossed in writing and research and end up sitting for many hours a day. That's why I take time every day, usually around the time I eat lunch, to do a set of stretches to stay limber.

Talking with my daughter: When I was working full-time, I was lucky if I got to speak to my daughter on a weekly basis. Being an introvert, I needed to reset and recharge when I got home from work, and talking to other people was difficult. Now that I am retired and working my dream job from home (no employees or customers), I look for ways to connect with people outside. Speaking with my daughter on her lunch hour or while she is driving home from work has become a cherished daily ritual.

Watching TV with my husband: This ritual is a lovely way to wind down from the day.

My Daily Schedule

Here's how my rituals fit into my regular daily schedule.

7:00 A.M.	Wake up, brush teeth and hair, wash face, etc.
7:15 A.M.	Make my morning green tea over ice with organic lemons and take my supplements. Say good morning to my husband and dog, who have already been up since 6:00.
7:30 A.M.	Head to the computer and check email, blogs, and social media.
9:30 A.M.	Depending on the day, I'll either continue working or run errands.
11:30 A.M. – 1:00 P.M.	At any point during this time, I might eat lunch and do some stretching. Figure out dinner and what I need to defrost, purchase, or prep.
1:00 P.M.	Back to the computer to do any pending work for the blogs. Check email, social media, etc.
4:30 P.M.	My daughter calls me on her way home from work. I turn on the robo-vacuum, feed and take out the dog, check my garden, brush the dog, and feed our bird.
5:00 – 7:00 P.M.	Shower and start prepping dinner. When my husband gets home, we watch the evening news together, eat dinner, and talk about his day or our plans to work on our properties.

7:00 – 7:30 P.M.	Clean kitchen and tidy house.
8:00 P.M.	Watch TV with husband or do paperwork for his business.
10:00 P.M.	Husband and dog go to bed so I can write for a few hours. This time of day is best for writing because I have no interruptions with phone calls or social media.
1:00 A.M.	Brush teeth and go to bed.

My day is full! You can see that my rituals happen alongside my work and general maintenance tasks, which is what makes them so important. They are woven into the fabric of my retired life.

Identifying Your Current Rituals

Think about the small moments in your daily life now—what happens between the tasks on your to-do list? Make a list below of your regular rituals, then mark whether they are habits you want to continue during retirement.

1. _____

   Continue ☐   Do Not Continue ☐

2. _____

   Continue ☐   Do Not Continue ☐

3. _____

   Continue ☐   Do Not Continue ☐

4. _____

   Continue ☐   Do Not Continue ☐

5. _____

   Continue ☐   Do Not Continue ☐

6. _____

   Continue ☐   Do Not Continue ☐

7. _____

   Continue ☐   Do Not Continue ☐

Are you happy with what your days look like? Do you feel a sense of fulfillment with the time you spend between responsibilities?

Crafting New Rituals

Not everyone will start a business in retirement, as I did, which can leave a lot of hours in the day. Instead, focus on your values and hobbies. Reference the lists you made in chapter 2 (see pages 33 to 57), then consider some of these example rituals:

- Crafting (and savoring) your morning/evening beverage
- Exercising daily, such as walking
- Journaling
- Listening to music
- Listening to podcasts or audiobooks
- Meditating
- Reading
- Solving crosswords or other puzzles or brain games
- Spending time with pets
- Talking daily with a friend

Your rituals may be the things you wish you had more time for, like checking in on a neighbor or walking to a destination you normally drive to. Remember: Rituals are different from hobbies, though they can certainly tie together. For example, if candle making is a hobby you adopt during retirement, a daily ritual may be burning one of those candles and taking a moment to appreciate the aroma.

On the next page, make a list of the new rituals you would like to incorporate into your daily retirement life. You can even include the approximate time frames you will use for your rituals if you already have an idea.

1. _____

2. _____

3. _____

4. _____

5. _____

6. _____

7. _____

8. _____

9. _____

10. _____

Revisit your rituals as you get closer to retiring. You might start implementing some of the things you want to do before you retire to see if they will work for you during retirement.

Just remember, this list will need to remain fluid. What I thought I wanted at 50 changed in a few years, and I realized that I now have time for things I never even thought to include in my regular life, like watching TV with my husband. It's always best to remain flexible and open to new ideas even when it comes to your daily routine.

Sissy, 64
Former Teacher, Charleston, South Carolina

"Retirement is where you can wake up in the morning and have everything done by 8:00 a.m."

Ongoing Enrichment

Ongoing enrichment means the consistent bettering of your retired life through purposeful, values-driven activities. Those activities look very different to each person, but one that seems to be pretty universal among seniors and retirees is continued education, which can include learning a new skill, language, or subject matter.

But before we talk about what you'll learn, determine *how* you'll learn. Knowing what type of learner you are—visual, auditory, or kinesthetic—will help guide you toward the paths of learning that will be most successful for you in retirement. Take the quiz to discover your style of learning.

What Type of Learner Are You?

There are three types of learning: visual, meaning you learn best by seeing information translated into demonstrations, graphs, or pictures; auditory, meaning you retain information best after it's been explained to you (and often after you repeat it back to comprehend); and kinesthetic, meaning you prefer a hands-on approach and like to learn through experimentation.

In these questions, choose the answer that best reflects you.

1. When I'm learning something new, I understand best when I
   a. Watch someone demonstrate
   b. Listen to an explanation
   c. Figure it out by trying

2. When I am reading instructions, I usually
   a. See what I am reading in my mind
   b. Sound out the words or hear the words in my mind
   c. Write out the word with my finger

3. When I am asked to give driving directions to someone, I
   a. Visualize the place I am going and then draw the directions out on paper
   b. Tell someone verbally how to get there
   c. Use my body and point as I give the directions

4. If I am trying to remember how to spell a word, I
   a. Check my spelling by writing it down
   b. Spell it out loud
   c. Trace the letters with my finger to visualize the word

5. When writing something, I
   a. Space out my letters neatly—good penmanship is important to me
   b. Say the words in my head as I write them
   c. Write with force to emphasize certain words

6. When I need to remember items to buy at the store, I
   a. Write down each item
   b. Say the list to myself over and over
   c. Count the items on each finger

7. When attending a lecture, I prefer speakers or professors who
   a. Use a screen or white board while they speak
   b. Are very animated
   c. Allow me to learn by doing an activity

8. When trying to focus on a specific task, I have a difficult time when
   a. There is a lot of activity or disorganization in the room
   b. There is a lot of talking or loud noises in the room
   c. I have to stay in one place for too long

9. When trying to solve a difficult problem, I
   a. Write the problem out using a diagram or drawing to see it more clearly
   b. Talk about the problem and its characteristics
   c. Move my body or move objects so I can focus

10. When using written instructions to put something together, I
    a. Read the instructions quietly while visualizing how the parts will work
    b. Read them out loud and talk to myself as I put the parts together
    c. Put the parts together myself, then read the instructions later if I need help

11. To keep from getting bored while I am waiting, I
    a. Observe my surroundings
    b. Talk or listen to others
    c. Move nearby objects around or shake my feet if I have to sit

12. If I have to give verbal directions or instructions to another person, I
    a. Summarize and keep it brief
    b. Make sure I give every detail
    c. Demonstrate and use my body to help explain

Total up the number of each letter you chose. The option with the highest number is the type of learner you are.

A = _____ B = _____ C = _____

Mostly As: Visual Learner

Visual learners absorb better when they can see, rather than hear, what they are learning. They would rather watch than read about how to do something. YouTube videos are great for visual learners.

Mostly Bs: Auditory Learner

Auditory learners are better at hearing the subject matter. The auditory learner would enjoy a lecture over reading a book. Podcasts, audiobooks, and radio shows are a great way to absorb new information.

Mostly Cs: Kinesthetic Learner

The kinesthetic learner incorporates new information best by doing. This type of learner struggles to sit still, so they learn best when actively participating. Learning to ride a bike by riding it is an example of kinesthetic learning. Kinesthetic learners are good at sports and the arts and learn on the go.

If your scores are similar across types, you may have more than one learning style. Try to identify your strongest style, but allow yourself to learn in multiple ways if you find one style too limiting.

What Should I Learn?

The simple act of retiring can make people feel like their learning days are behind them, but the unfortunate truth is relaxing too much in retirement can bring on cognitive decline as well as depression (according to a 2019 study by the IZA Institute of Labor Economics). When you make a choice to learn in retirement, you are choosing to stay intellectually viable.

We have discussed what hobbies and activities you might like to do during retirement; now we will explore how you can use this time to expand your knowledge. College courses or online classes are a great way to explore new topics and even meet people to expand your social circle.

Here are some suggestions for new things to learn:

◆ Arts and crafts

◆ Computer skills

◆ Cooking and baking

◆ Dance

◆ New languages

◆ New sports

For this exercise, write down three new skills you would like to learn. Keeping your learning style in mind, research a few places where you can potentially learn each skill. It could be through a community center, podcast, online class, or educational center like a high school, tech school, or college. Also investigate government programs available through your local libraries, recreation centers, and adult education programs.

1. Skill: _____

   a. _____

   b. _____

   c. _____

2. Skill: _____

   a. _____

   b. _____

   c. _____

3. Skill: _____

    a. _____

    b. _____

    c. _____

Learning Institution Resources

Many seniors are returning to school as a way to stay active and engaged with life. Doing so helps many find a sense of purpose in their retirement. Often, seniors struggle with the loss of their social life from leaving their careers. Going back to a campus can fill that missing piece. There are several options to choose from, and many are free or come at a significantly reduced rate.

Coursera

Coursera offers free online courses from professors at major universities like Stanford and Duke. If you are willing to pay, you can also earn a certificate in those courses, a great option for those earlier in retirement who want to boost their retirement résumé. Hundreds of free courses allow you to view video lectures and do homework. Paid courses provide additional quizzes and projects for the certificate. Starting at just $39, they are affordable for almost everyone. You can view the impressive and comprehensive list of high-level courses on Coursera's website, coursera.org.

The Oasis Institute

The Oasis Institute was founded in St. Louis, Missouri, with the mission "to promote healthy aging through life-long learning, active lifestyles, and volunteer engagement."

Oasis programs reach more than 250 communities with traditional learning as well as peer-led classes hosted by volunteers. There are several categories to choose from and hundreds of classes in which seniors can pursue a wide variety of interests, such as:

- Arts and entertainment

- Exercise

- History

- Practical

- Technology

- Wellness

The Oasis Institute has a national network in over 22 states, but also offers online classes, so location is not an issue. You can find its locations listed on the website (oasisnet.org/locations), or if you are interested in online classes, review the offerings at oasiseverywhere.org.

Osher Lifelong Learning Institute

The Bernard Osher Foundation continually supports more than 100 learning programs at colleges all over the United States. These courses are for people over 50 who are interested in continuing their education without grades, homework, or exams. Colleges can offer the courses at low (or even no) cost for seniors who are interested in pursuing higher education for the joy of learning and enriching their lives. They offer courses in the arts, film, history, and even finance. Look on the website, osherfoundation.org, for the institutes offered.

Many seniors may be looking to complete their college degree. If doing so is your goal, contact your local college and ask if they offer waivers to seniors pursuing their degree later in life. There will be age and possibly financial requirements to qualify. Usually schools will offer the tuition waivers to folks over 60. Many schools offer open seats to seniors if seats remain after full-time students have enrolled. Professors often like having the more mature point of view added to the discussion in the classroom setting, so you will be a welcome presence.

Kathy, 59
Pastor's Wife, Aiken, South Carolina

"Starting a blog was one of the hardest things I ever had to do. I had no idea what I was getting into! I was completely new to technology, and building my own website seemed like an impossible task. But I persevered, took classes, and found other new bloggers who helped each other out."

How to Create a Positive Learning Environment in Retirement

The thought of learning new skills can be daunting to those going into retirement. Maybe you are ready for relaxation and looking forward to your daily life getting easier. But as we discussed earlier, a life of total leisure can take a toll on your emotional and intellectual health over time. A happy retirement is one with leisure, yes, but also one with intention and purpose, which can be spurred by a positive learning environment. Here are 10 ways to create or maintain that positive learning environment:

1. **Maintain relationships with like-minded positive people.** I learned early on that being around negative, unproductive people kept me from having an open mind and pursuing new ideas. Make sure you are keeping toxic people at a distance.

2. **Work to let go of fears.** If someone else can do it, you can, too. Push through your fears and try something new. You might be surprised at how achievable it is.

3. **Serve others.** Helping others often helps us learn more about ourselves and teaches us leadership and teamwork because we are in a positive environment. Motivational speaker Zig Ziglar said, "You can have everything in life you want, if you will just help other people get what they want."

4. **Commit to becoming a lifelong learner.** When thinking of different learning activities to pursue, replace the word "if" with "when." "If" projects doubt.

5. **Start using the phrase "I get to" versus "I have to."**

6. **Replace negative thoughts with positive beliefs.** For every negative thought you have, write down the opposite positive thought and memorize it. I often put positive quotations around my house so I can read them daily.

7. **Live in the now.** Focusing on the past or even fantasizing about the future robs us of what we have right in front of us today, causing us to miss out!

8. **Practice gratitude.** When we are focused on the things we have, we are less likely to notice what we do not have.

9. **Learn from others.** Listen to podcasts, take classes, or read books by motivational speakers that focus on personal growth.

10. **Love yourself.** Learning new things is an act of self-love that will help you connect deeper with yourself and build wisdom.

Kevin, 52
Former Banker, Toronto, Canada

"Retirement is not the end of something but the beginning of a new journey, and you get to decide the path."

Part III

Living Your Best Life

In the next chapters, you will dig into understanding your personality. With a clear understanding of self, you can better connect your retirement aspirations with ways to best achieve them. Understanding your personality will also help keep you from becoming disillusioned during retirement while maintaining a level of flexible freedom.

CHAPTER 6

Your Fullest Self

Just as knowing what kind of learner you are can help you determine how to approach your ongoing education in retirement, understanding your personality type can drive your focus in choosing purposeful activities. In this chapter, you will explore your personality traits to find out what gives you a sense of peace and belonging.

Before you start the quizzes that follow, review your answers from chapter 2, where you identified your values, inspirations, and hobbies (see pages 33 to 57). Your quiz results will tie into everything you have learned so far.

The Physical Self

The physical self includes our outward appearance, our endurance, and our mental stamina. When we bring the three together in harmony, our bodies operate like a well-oiled machine. This quiz will help you identify the physical properties on which to focus so you can meet your goals.

1. Which is most likely to be found in your home?
    a. Weights
    b. A full vanity
    c. Tinctures

2. How long is your morning routine?
    a. 1 hour
    b. 2+ hours
    c. 15 minutes

3. When working out, you would rather be in:
    a. A group class outdoors
    b. A local gym
    c. Your home

4. You find yourself mainly making goals:
    a. For the short term
    b. For the long term
    c. Day by day

5. On a bad day, what is your biggest challenge?
    a. Being physically active
    b. Controlling negative thoughts or emotions
    c. Eating well

6. Where do you notice stress first?

   a. In your muscles and joints
   b. In your attitude
   c. In your thoughts

7. Which result excites you the most?

   a. Completing a race that you previously could not
   b. Seeing results from an exercise program
   c. Noticing your health improve with dietary changes

8. To what extent does your mental state impact your physical being?

   a. Somewhat
   b. Barely
   c. Greatly

9. Which type of competition are you most likely to participate in?

   a. A weightlifting competition
   b. A triathlon
   c. A 5k

10. How would you dress for an active day?

    a. Performance or compression wear
    b. Tank top and shorts
    c. Sweatsuit

Scoring Guide

For every **A**, give yourself **1 point**.
For every **B**, give yourself **2 points**.
For every **C**, give yourself **3 points**.

Total _____

If you scored 10 to 15 points, you focus on **PERFORMANCE**. When you think about your physical being, you see a machine that was designed to do incredible things. You also know that your body, much like a machine, requires maintenance and recalibration to function to its highest ability. You are competitive and always strive for excellence. You take pride in knowing you are in optimal condition.

If you scored 16 to 23 points, you focus on **PERFECTION**. Your body is your temple, and you have a blueprint for how you want that temple to look. You take time and consideration in perfecting your outward appearance to accurately resemble how you feel inside. You feel your absolute best when you can synchronize the two.

If you scored 24 to 30 points, you focus on **NOURISHMENT**. You see your body as more than just a temple or a machine; it is your home. You like to make sure your physical home is in order, but you are less concerned with perfecting your appearance than you are about taking care of your overall health. Everything about your body, from what you eat to the work you put into it, has a specific purpose in creating your ideal physical environment.

The Social Self

With so many new ways to connect today, identifying and fine-tuning your social self is key. This quiz will help you assess your strengths and weaknesses and offer some suggestions to make your social life soar.

1. Where do you go when arriving at a party?
   a. Toward the first friendly face
   b. Toward the food and drink
   c. To find the host

2. In your circle of friends, you typically:
   a. Change plans
   b. Avoid plans altogether or show up only sometimes
   c. Make plans

3. In high school, which superlative would you have been likely to receive?
   a. Class clown
   b. Best smile
   c. Most likely to succeed

4. How often do you find yourself complimenting others?
   a. Very often
   b. Rarely
   c. Often

5. When you see an old friend in a public setting, you:
   a. Approach them
   b. Text them later to say that you thought you saw them
   c. Try to make eye contact so they approach you

6. Sensing a conversation is beginning to stall, you:
   a. Look for someone new to talk to
   b. Excuse yourself before it can end uncomfortably
   c. Ask questions to bring it back to life

7. When conversing in a group, you are most likely to:
   a. Insert a humorous anecdote
   b. Share only when spoken to directly
   c. Begin a debate

8. You would feel most comfortable meeting a friend at:
   a. An outdoor festival
   b. A local coffee shop
   c. Home

9. Which plans would you be least likely to cancel?
   a. Dining in a murder mystery theater
   b. Attending a gallery opening
   c. Taking a guided tour of a winery

10. What is your favorite part of a celebration or holiday?
    a. Gathering around the table with loved ones
    b. Catching up with friends and family one on one
    c. The excitement of preparing for guests

Scoring Guide

For every **A**, give yourself **1 point**.
For every **B**, give yourself **2 points**.
For every **C**, give yourself **3 points**.

Total _____

If you scored 10 to 15 points, you are a **SOCIAL BUTTERFLY**. You enjoy interaction with many diverse groups of people. Finding new restaurants and exploring new venues brings you great joy that spreads to everyone around you. Checking out some local social clubs and high-energy organizations that offer volunteer opportunities, such as Habitat for Humanity or Boys and Girls Club, would be extremely fulfilling and could provide more opportunities to showcase your vibrance in retirement.

If you scored 16 to 23 points, you are a **FLY ON THE WALL**. You thrive in large or small groups, as long as you are kept well out of the spotlight. You feel comfortable offering ideas and commentary on your own terms, but you prefer to sit back and observe the dynamics of the crowd. Your social type could also benefit from joining a social club for a hobby or sport you enjoy in retirement, but nothing that demands too much of your time or places you in a position of authority.

If you scored 24 to 30 points, you are a **RINGLEADER**. With your effortless ability to plan and unite, you prefer small groups where you can oversee an activity and ensure that everyone's needs are met. You thrive on entertaining guests and fostering intimate and meaningful connections with others. Hosting a book club or wine tasting is right up your retirement alley.

The Creative Self

Every brain uses unique methods to create. This quiz will help you identify your creative type so you can best use your individual strengths when you begin a creative venture.

1. When working on a group project, you prefer to:
   a. Present the idea and let others complete the project
   b. Be responsible for a specific objective
   c. Be the leader and assign individual roles

2. You are given a blank piece of paper. What do you do with it?
   a. Begin to doodle
   b. Make a paper airplane
   c. Start writing down ideas or journaling

3. What is your favorite part of creative expression?
   a. Creating something to share with the world
   b. Bringing your ideas to life
   c. Your relationship with the methods you use

4. How do you respond to criticism of your work?
   a. Decide not to create in that way again
   b. Accept the criticism and apply it to future work
   c. Receive the input but stand firm in your art

5. When traveling, you care most about:
   a. The destination
   b. The route
   c. The budget

6. Where are you most comfortable?
   a. Alone
   b. In small groups
   c. Among large crowds

7. What would you rather be known for?
   a. Your philanthropy
   b. Writing a bestseller
   c. Setting a world record

8. Your workspace is:
   a. Cluttered
   b. Depends on the day
   c. Neat

9. What is your biggest pet peeve when working with others?
   a. Not having enough creative freedom
   b. Lazy partners
   c. Someone taking credit for your work

10. Which activity best helps you brainstorm?
    a. Meditating
    b. Outlining
    c. Exercising

Scoring Guide

For every **A**, give yourself **1 point**.
For every **B**, give yourself **2 points**.
For every **C**, give yourself **3 points**.

Total _____

If you scored 10 to 15 points, you might be a **DREAMER**. Dreamers are easily swept away by their ideas and often have multiple projects in development at any given moment. As a dreamer, you enjoy the process almost more than the destination and need to be held accountable by creative partners and friends to help stay focused and complete your work. However, when you do finish, the result is intricate and beautiful because you tended to it at length and nurtured it into existence.

If you scored 16 to 23 points, you might be a **THINKER**. Thinkers see creative projects as problems to be solved and strive to find a variety of ways to solve them. You carefully plan your methods of execution to find the best possible way to share your ideas with the world. You might have a harder time starting your projects but are quick to finish because you already know the most efficient path to completion.

If you scored 24 to 30 points, you might be a **PRODUCER**. Producers have a variety of creative strengths and are used best in leadership roles. Collaborative projects are the most appealing to you given your ability to delegate responsibilities and unite others toward a singular goal. As a producer, you need help seeing your creative works as intellectual pieces of art that carry a message rather than just well-laid-out plans.

The Adventurous Self

We all crave adventure. Some of us seek it in the outdoors, some in the corners of our minds, and others in our relationships and careers. This quiz highlights your avenue of adventure and reveals how best to keep yourself on your toes in retirement.

1. Which would you most want to discover?
   a. An ancient civilization
   b. A cure for a terminal illness
   c. A new species of animal

2. In your day to day, what is most important?
   a. Fun
   b. Stability
   c. Growth

3. You arrive at your campsite. What do you do first?
   a. Start a fire
   b. Set up your tent
   c. Explore the area

4. On a cruise, which excursion would you most look forward to?
   a. Horseback riding on the beach
   b. Touring a historical site
   c. Swimming with dolphins

5. For which innovator would you want to be an apprentice?
   a. Elon Musk
   b. Alexander Graham Bell
   c. Leonardo da Vinci

6. In what area do you think the next great scientific revelation will take place?
   a. Space exploration
   b. Renewable energy sources
   c. Deep sea exploration

7. If you could be proficient in one skill, what would it be?
   a. Public speaking
   b. Carpentry
   c. Celestial navigation

8. What has stopped you from taking your dream vacation?
   a. Career limitations
   b. Family responsibilities
   c. Financial obligations

9. You never leave home without:
   a. Your wallet
   b. An itinerary
   c. Your cell phone

10. Which trilogy do you find the most exciting?
    a. *Indiana Jones*
    b. *The Matrix*
    c. *Lord of the Rings*

Scoring Guide

For every **A**, give yourself **1 point**.
For every **B**, give yourself **2 points**.
For every **C**, give yourself **3 points**.

Total _____

If you scored 10 to 15 points, you might be a **RISK TAKER**. In your search for excitement, you are aware of risks but are stimulated by the thought of conquering them. Although you might have to remind yourself on occasion that some risks are greater than others, you charge ahead confidently knowing that the outcome is not always the most important. You also appreciate learning from past mistakes. You might even find satisfaction simply by evaluating risk and pressing forward.

If you scored 16 to 23 points, you might be a **MANIFESTER**. Your dreams quickly become your reality. You see no obstacle you cannot overcome, and the journey excites you. "Determined" is an adjective commonly used to describe your persistence, and you effectively strategize how best to accomplish your objectives. Always seeking the next best thing, you apply your adventurous spirit to every goal, destination, and career move.

If you scored 24 to 30 points, you might be an **EXPLORER**. Inspiration, for you, comes from exploring every corner of the earth. Every road traveled, path crossed, or mountain climbed symbolizes a deeper connection to your place in time. Eagerness and optimism are your strengths, and your weaknesses are only what you allow to hold yourself back from the adventures the world has to offer. Get out there!

The Intellectual Self

Intellectuality isn't so much a measurement of "smarts" as it is an evaluation of how you process information and reason with your actions or emotions. This quiz will help you identify how to keep your intellect alive.

1. In grade school, which came easiest for you?
   a. Reading
   b. Mathematics
   c. Writing

2. When debating an unfamiliar issue, you:
   a. Continue to debate, and base your opinion on a similar issue
   b. Decline to comment until you have researched independently
   c. Freeze up

3. In social settings, you are most likely to:
   a. Present deep discussion topics
   b. Only converse with those close to you
   c. Observe the environment and avoid interaction

4. When given an assignment, you typically spend more time:
   a. Researching
   b. Revising
   c. Outlining

5. When a solicitor calls, you typically:
   a. Hang up immediately
   b. Listen to their pitch and ask questions
   c. Give support to their cause

6. An opinion is presented to you through a trusted media outlet. You:
   a. Accept the opinion and repeat it as fact
   b. Research other opinions and form your own
   c. Completely disregard it

7. You have fallen ill and are discussing treatment options with your doctor. You are more likely to:
   a. Accept the initial suggested treatment or medications
   b. Seek a second opinion before deciding
   c. Decline treatment in hopes of a homeopathic remedy

8. If your car needs a repair, you would first ask the opinion of:
   a. The dealership
   b. A local mechanic
   c. A friend

9. A friend is upset over a troubled relationship. Your advice to them is:
   a. To weigh the pros and cons
   b. To reflect inward
   c. To remain optimistic

10. Whom would you consider to be wiser?
   a. A billionaire mogul
   b. A tenured college professor
   c. A Nobel Prize winner

Scoring Guide

For every **A**, give yourself **1 point**.
For every **B**, give yourself **2 points**.
For every **C**, give yourself **3 points**.

Total _____

If you scored 10 to 15 points, you use your intellect to **INFER**. When you are given information, you make conclusions based on your own reasoning of what has been presented. You stand firm and do not let others' opinions easily influence you. To you, facts tend to be black and white, and results are direct outcomes of the circumstances that produced them. This method of reasoning comes into play in your relationships, too. Your close friends are those who directly attribute to your happiness and who serve a solid purpose. No room for wishy-washy people here!

If you scored 16 to 23 points, you use your intellect to **INTERPRET**. As an intellectual interpreter, you base your decisions not only on the facts presented but also on what you perceive lies underneath those facts. You do not jump to conclusions based on face value; you carefully dissect the issues at hand and determine what might have led to this point. Whereas some are quick to dismiss others who disagree, you are willing to get to the core of others' opinions and try to find common ground that benefits both sides.

If you scored 24 to 30 points, you use your intellect to **IMAGINE**. You see beyond established facts and the reasoning behind scientific theories. You use your intellect not only to gather and question the information at your fingertips, but also to further hypothesize scenarios that could disprove or expand on what we know of the world. Visionaries who share an imaginative intellect are essential as we move forward in exploration of different solar systems and the hidden corners of our own great planet.

The Spiritual Self

Spirituality encompasses far more than your religious beliefs and affiliation. It can be a driving force that guides you through tough decisions or hardship, and it must be nurtured just like your physical form. This quiz will help you pinpoint the best way to solidify and support your spiritual self.

1. How do you prefer to spend your free time?
    a. Reading
    b. In nature
    c. Volunteering

2. When others seek your help, it is typically for:
    a. Your advice on an issue
    b. Financial support
    c. Help with a project

3. Which is currently a main focus of your life?
   a. Expanding your knowledge in a particular area
   b. Identifying your purpose
   c. Improving your relationships with family and friends

4. After being in a large group for an extended period, you feel:
   a. Anxious
   b. Exhausted
   c. Energized

5. How do you normally rejuvenate your mind and body?
   a. Take a spa day
   b. Nap
   c. Exercise

6. After an argument with a loved one, you are most likely to:
   a. Give them space and let them contact you when they're ready
   b. Fixate on the negative emotion
   c. Apologize immediately

7. Which is a guiding force in your life?
   a. Seeking truth
   b. Living up to your highest potential
   c. Making connections and finding love

8. Whose advice are you most likely to take?
   a. A religious leader
   b. A self-help expert
   c. A trusted friend

9. You consider yourself to be more of a(n):

   a. Realist
   b. Empath
   c. Intellectual

10. Which activity would you get the most fulfillment from?

    a. Attending a lecture or TED Talk
    b. Yoga
    c. Mentoring youth

Scoring Guide

For every **A**, give yourself **1 point**.
For every **B**, give yourself **2 points**.
For every **C**, give yourself **3 points**.

Total _____

If you scored 10 to 15 points, you might benefit from **STUDYING**. For you, growth is most important, and any use of your time is evaluated on the potential growth you could achieve from it. No matter the topic, truths can be learned that can also identify areas of your life that could use strengthening. As you grow, you are also more apt to help others in their spiritual walks. The more you learn about yourself, others, and the world around you, the deeper the connection you will feel to your spiritual self.

If you scored 16 to 23 points, you might benefit from **MEDITATION**. Your spirit requires a little more tender loving care than others, mainly because it exhausts itself quickly tending to the emotional needs of those closest to you. Meditation can prove to be a powerful reset button, lifting negative emotion as well as physical stress from your shoulders. Meditation is time for you to relax, reflect, pray, and plan before you take on a new day.

If you scored 24 to 30 points, you might benefit from **WORKS**. You tend to be more selfless in your approach to emboldening your spirituality, always giving to others and offering a helping hand. By volunteering and assisting those in need, you are consistently broadening your empathy, compassion, and positive connection to the world around you. Everyone has distinct skills and purposes, and you might have known yours for some time now. By sharing your gifts with others, you leave a positive impact in the world that only you can.

Putting All Your Selves Together

How can you use your strengths in your daily pursuit of purpose during retirement? List each of your quiz results below and, using the descriptions for each answer and your previous exercises throughout part 1, brainstorm the top three ways you can satisfy your needs. As an example, the result for my spiritual self was "studying." Finding a spiritual study group might help me satisfy that part of my personality. Or I could take a class on the history of the world's religions or listen to podcasts from top theologians. The possibilities are endless!

Physical Self Result: _____

1. _____

2. _____

3. _____

Social Self Result: _____

1. _____
2. _____
3. _____

Creative Self Result: _____

1. _____
2. _____
3. _____

Adventurous Self Result: _____

1. _____
2. _____
3. _____

Intellectual Self Result: _____

1. _____
2. _____
3. _____

Spiritual Self Result: _____

1. _____
2. _____
3. _____

CHAPTER 7

The Bigger Picture

At this point, you have done the work and mapped out your plan for retirement. Now you'll want to reflect on the details and use them to understand how you will have an impact on your community, region, and even the rest of the world.

Your Community

Deciding where you will live in retirement is one of the key factors in crafting your particular retirement lifestyle. Whether you are staying in your current home or relocating, you will need to decide how much to participate in your local community, which starts with evaluating what that community has to offer retirees.

Florida usually dominates the lists of top places to retire, but it's not the only American state with a warm, tropical climate. Folks often investigate Texas and other Southern states like Georgia and South Carolina. Others make the move to Mexico, Costa Rica, or Belize because of cost of living considerations.

In this exercise, we will map out where you want to live. You will first choose a general region, then delve into the nuances of that region to find your perfect landing spot. Refer back to chapter 2 where you listed your values, hobbies, and interests (see pages 33 to 57) so you can ensure your location will meet those needs. For example, if surfing is one of your hobbies, you would not want to choose the mountains of Colorado.

Choose Your Region

Consider the following questions to determine the best region for your retirement life.

1. What kind of climate do I want to live in?

   _____

2. Which U.S. states and which countries provide that climate?

   _____

3. What is the cost of living in each of these areas?

_____

_____

4. Will I be able to travel easily to see friends and family? Is there a nearby airport that can accommodate my travel needs?

_____

_____

5. What are the tax consequences of choosing any of these areas? (Some states may charge state income tax or have higher sales, fuel, and property taxes.)

_____

_____

6. What are the health care consequences of choosing any of these areas? Will I have to get additional health benefits?

_____

_____

7. Is the quality of life what I am accustomed to? Are there environmental deficiencies that will be of concern?

_____

_____

Choose Your City or Town

Now, zero in on a few areas. If you chose Florida, consider coastal area, like the panhandle, and inland areas. I live on the Treasure Coast of Florida. The area is comparatively rural, but many Florida cities are between one and three hours away, providing an easy commute to airports. It is coastal and offers many cultural activities, such as theaters, museums, and music venues.

Within your chosen area, look at three or four towns that might interest you.

1. _____

    a. _____

    b. _____

    c. _____

    d. _____

2. _____

    a. _____

    b. _____

    c. _____

    d. _____

3. _____

    a. _____

    b. _____

    c. _____

    d. _____

Next, use these questions to help you decide between the smaller areas you've identified.

1. What medical services and health care facilities are available? Check into hospitals, medical networks, and long-term care facilities. How are they rated?

2. Is your health insurance accepted in this area by enough medical professionals that you have choices?

3. What senior services are available? Look into senior transportation, meal and errand assistance, Visiting Nurses Association (VNA), and hospice.

4. Are your desired retirement hobbies easily accessible in these areas? For example, do you have access to water sports or mountains? Is there an arts community that offers classes? Are there clubs specific to your hobby?

5. What does the cultural scene look like? Are there museums, art galleries, or a community theater?

6. What entertainment venues are available? Are there plenty of community events, like downtown Friday Festivals or concerts?

7. What are the housing costs? Is there a nearby town that offers lower home prices? Are there low-maintenance options available? What is the property tax millage rate? What are the insurance costs?

8. Will you be able to pursue your spiritual journey here? Is there a local church or spiritual center that meets your needs?

9. Are there plenty of volunteer opportunities?

10. Is the area too touristy? Are there seasonal fluctuations in residents and visitors?

11. Are any professional or even amateur sports offered? Many retirees enjoy going to high school sports games.

12. Many people will rent when they first move to an area to make sure it is a good fit before they buy. What is the rental market like? Will you be able to find a rental that suits your needs, accepts pets, etc.?

13. Is the area pet-friendly? Are there dog parks, pet-friendly beaches or trails, and restaurants for you to take your dog to?

14. Are your values being represented by the community? Are there initiatives in place for economic development, the environment, or social justice that you can participate in?

15. If you wish to further your education, are in-person classes available that meet your needs?

Lanora, 66
Former Dermatologist, Massapequa, New York

"Volunteering for your community is more of a gift for you than anyone else."

The World

Next, we will map out your global plans. How do you plan to engage with the global community? Often, new retirees will take a trip to a foreign land. However, that is not the only option available when you are considering how to connect with the rest of the world.

You might want to move to a foreign country to experience the world, or seek volunteer opportunities for retirees who are looking to find new challenges outside the United States. Let's explore both options.

Becoming an Expat

More than 431,000 American retirees are currently living abroad and receiving social security benefits. This tendency has become very popular because the cost of living can be significantly lower in other countries, allowing for a better lifestyle.

Every January, *International Living* (InternationalLiving.com) releases a report of the 10 best international places to retire, derived from surveys completed by expats living the dream abroad.

There are 10 categories you should evaluate when considering other countries to live in:

1. **Assimilation:** Are locals open to U.S. expats moving there? Are you open to local customs?

2. **Climate:** Is the climate mild or severe? Does it suit your hobbies?

3. **Cost of living:** Are food, utilities, and other daily expenses higher or lower than what you currently pay?

4. **Discounts and benefits for seniors:** Look for tax and medical exemptions for seniors.

5. **Ease of entry, visas, and work permits:** Is the country receptive to U.S. expats coming to the area?

6. **Entertainment:** Is there safe and inexpensive entertainment available?

7. **Housing:** Is the housing more affordable when you consider all the costs of living in this region?

8. **Language barriers:** Are you willing to learn the language? Are there English-speaking people around to help you get by until you pick up the language?

9. **Quality of healthcare:** Is there quality healthcare with advanced equipment for seniors?

10. **Stability of the government:** Is there widespread corruption or unrest in any parts of the region?

Nancy, 64
Former Administrative Assistant, Madrid, Spain

"Moving to Spain was a challenge. I had to learn a new language and adapt to the culture. However, in Australia, I could never enjoy the quality of life I have in Spain. I would not have been able to retire at all."

Volunteering Overseas

Several companies facilitate opportunities for retirees to work with ethical and responsible groups overseas. Here are a few types of volunteer opportunities you might consider:

- Animal welfare and conservancy
- Diversification programs
- Environmental programs
- Faith-Based programs
- Farming and agriculture

- Homelessness, construction, and remodeling
- Professional services
- Teaching and educational services

Joining these programs does have a cost, but some expenses are included. The costs and offerings vary greatly, with fees ranging from as little as $199 per week into the thousands for longer stays and more sought-after destinations. Consider these example trips from ProjectsAbroad (projects-abroad.com), which are strictly for people over 50.

Conservation and Community Work in Ecuador

- Fixed dates throughout the year
- Anyone age 50 or over can join
- Starts at two weeks
- From $3,605 USD

Childcare Volunteering in Nepal

- Fixed dates throughout the year
- Anyone age 50 or over can join
- Starts at two weeks
- From $2,305 USD

Lower-cost programs typically have additional fees not included in the cost of the program. Here are some of the charges and expenses you might also be responsible for:

- Airfare
- Criminal background checks
- Language lessons

- Mandatory travel insurance

- Meals

- Tours

- Transportation transfer to the airport at the conclusion of the program

- Vaccinations

- Visa

One of my favorite blogs, *Over 50 and Overseas* (Over50AndOverseas.com), offers vetted resources for volunteer travel opportunities. This blog will help guide you through the process of deciding where to best put your resources.

Joining the Peace Corps

If you are looking for a more committed role volunteering globally or do not have the funds to pay for volunteer vacation programs, you may want to consider the Peace Corps. They offer volunteer opportunities in more than 60 countries and provide a small stipend to offset expenses, transportation, health insurance, and housing. They even offer a bonus to help you acclimate back home once your tour is complete.

The Peace Corps is not just for younger folks—it has opportunities for all ages. Many retirees commit to working for the organization for two years when they initially retire. However, the Peace Corps is not for the faint of heart. You will be living in similar conditions as the people you are serving. That can mean no air-conditioning and sharing a bathroom. However, the rewards far outweigh the difficulties.

David, 67
Former University Administrator, Durham,
North Carolina

"My wife, Champa, and I joined the Peace Corps when we
were 63 years old, serving in Moldova, a former Soviet
state located between Ukraine and Romania. Our post
was in a small city near the capital, where we lived with
a wonderful family. Champa taught English at the school,
and I worked at the library, helping the administra-
tors launch new classes, update their communications,
and create a beautiful family room. We had an amaz-
ing experience, which I describe in my book, Not Exactly
Retired: A Life-Changing Journey on the Road and in the
Peace Corps.*"*

Your Passion Project

Many of us have passions we've had to put on the back burner
because of career and family. Not just hobbies, these are the
projects that truly reflect our aspirations and values—those
we would be remiss to say we never completed in our life-
times, such as writing a memoir or learning to fly a plane.
Retirement is the perfect time to pursue that passion project.
It is also a great way to replace a career that took up much of
your time.

If you are not quite sure what you are most passionate
about, the exercise below will help set up an initial framework
to get you started. You can also refer to your commandments,
values, and hobbies lists in chapter 2 (see pages 33 to 57) to
help. But the goal here is to find what you are *most* passionate
about and brings you the most excitement.

The Things I Care Most About

Write down three things you are passionate about. They might be family oriented, like caring for grandchildren, or community oriented, like building low-income housing. They might be related to personal growth.

1. _____

2. _____

3. _____

Three Things I Can Do Today to Support My Passion

Choose the item from the list above you are most drawn to. What are the next steps to bring your passion project to fruition? Is it gathering information about volunteer opportunities? Starting the outline for your novel? Write down the first three actions you can take to set your project in motion.

Passion Project: _____

1. _____

2. _____

3. _____

Set Up Goals and a Schedule of To-Dos

Your days during retirement can start to fill up just as quickly as your working days, and your passion project may still be waiting in the background. Plan for your project early in retirement before other priorities take over.

Here you'll set up time frames and goals for the first 90 days of your project. It could be gathering the information you need to get started, creating a business plan, organizing applications for volunteer work, getting travel documents in order, or starting a website.

For each month below, write down your overall goal, or how much progress you would like to have made by that point. Then list five steps you need to take to make that monthly goal a reality.

Month One

Overall Goal: _____

Steps

1. _____

2. _____

3. _____

4. _____

5. _____

Month Two

Overall Goal: _____

Steps

1. _____

2. _____

3. _____

4. _____

5. _____

Month Three

Overall Goal: _____

Steps

1. _____

2. _____

3. _____

4. _____

5. _____

Putting pen to paper makes it easier to work through your ideas and helps bring them to fruition. Finding a passion project is not totally necessary in retirement, but it does help expand your feelings of purpose and replace the routine of a career.

Pat, 79
Former Headhunter, Virginia Beach, Virginia

"Retirement is the time when you realize you spent too many years not pursuing your dreams and also when you realize it is never too late!"

Conclusion

After all the exercises, questions, budgets, and quizzes in this book, you should be ready to embark on your retirement journey. If you are not completely settled in all your decisions for retirement, that's okay! Remember that just as every individual is different, so is every retirement experience. One of my main goals for retirement was to experience as many new things as I could, even if I didn't think a particular activity was in my wheelhouse. Don't let fears or insecurities guide your decisions.

If at any point you are feeling stuck during retirement, come back and review your answers to reflect on who you are and where you want to go. Stay true to the goals you have set for yourself and for your retirement, but remain open and flexible to new ideas. Doing so will keep you balanced and centered. When you are financially, emotionally, and spiritually prepared as you enter this last leg of your journey, your retirement will bring you great satisfaction.

Resources

AARP

This organization provides resources for seniors looking to get more out of their retirement. AARP.org has a 401(k) calculator tool, AARP.org/work/retirement-planning /401k_calculator.html.

Born to Be Boomers

This lifestyle blog, borntobeboomers.com, helps people over 50 looking to make the most out of life.

International Living

An online magazine, InternationalLiving.com, for prospective expats.

The Retirement and IRA Show

This retirement podcast, TheRetirementAndIRAShow .com, offers financial advice.

Retirement Starts Today Radio

Benjamin Brandt hosts this popular retirement podcast, RetirementStartsTodayRadio.com.

Sara Zeff Geber, PhD

Dr. Geber specializes in helping people transition into solo retirement, SaraZeffGeber.com.

Social Security Website

Provides retirement calculators and other important information about social security benefits, SSA.gov.

USA.gov Retirement Website

This government website, USA.gov/retirement, answers common questions about retirement and social security.

References

Arias, Elizabeth, and Jiaquan Xu. "United States Life Tables, 2017." National Center for Health Statistics. *National Vital Statistics Reports* 68, no. 7 (June 24, 2019). CDC.gov /nchs/data/nvsr/nvsr68/nvsr68_07-508.pdf.

Eisenberg, Richard. "Expat Retirees Reveal How Life Has Turned Out." *Forbes.* July 30, 2015. Forbes.com/sites /nextavenue/2015/07/30/expat-retirees-reveal-how -life-has-turned-out/?sh=5c8f375b1879.

Jarmul, David. *Not Exactly Retired: A Life-Changing Journey on the Road and in the Peace Corps.* Oakland, CA: A Peace Corps Writers Book, 2020.

Mansfield, Mike, and Lex Van Delden. "Successful Retirement—Healthy Aging and Financial Security." Aegon Center for Longevity and Retirement. November 16, 2017. Aegon.com/contentassets/ee40839bdaa 1486484f924b31d02618d/life-insurance-and-pensions -conference.pdf.

Muoio, Danielle. "Japan is running out of people to take care of the elderly, so it's making robots instead." *Business Insider.* November 20, 2015. BusinessInsider .com/japan-developing-carebots-for-elderly-care -2015-11#:~:text=To%20address%20the%20issue%2C%20 Japanese,is%20allocated%20to%20developing%20 carebots.

Plamen, Nikolov, and Alan Adelman. "IZA DP No. 12524: Do Pension Benefits Accelerate Cognitive Decline? Evidence from Rural China." IZA Institute of Labor Economics. August 2019. IZA.org/en/publications/dp/12524 /do-pension-benefits-accelerate-cognitive-decline -evidence-from-rural-china.

Social Security Administration, Office of Retirement and
Disability Policy. "Annual Statistical Supplement, 2020."
Accessed October 20, 2020. SSA.gov/policy/docs
/statcomps/supplement/2020/5j.html#table5.j11.

Umeda, Sayuri. "Japan: Foreign Caregivers Will Soon Be Able
to Work in Japan." Library of Congress Law. *Global Legal
Monitor*. December 27, 2016. LOC.gov/law/foreign-news
/article/japan-foreign-caregivers-will-soon-be-able
-to-work-in-japan/#:~:text=By%202025%2C%20all%20
Japanese%20baby,shortage%20of%20caregivers%20
for%20them.

Index

P

R

S

T

V

Acknowledgments

I want to thank my husband of 25 years, Jack, for putting up with and supporting me through all my endeavors. I would also like to acknowledge our daughter Kate, who has been not only a wonderful support in starting my writing career but also the best friend a mom could ever ask for. Thank you both for supporting me and my crazy ideas!

About the Author

Tricia Ryan Snow worked in the financial services and banking industry for more than 20 years before deciding to divorce the corporate world in 2018. She retired early so she could travel with her husband, Jack Snow (the Boomer), and their dog, Bo. They enjoy finding new experiences together. Tricia runs the popular lifestyle blog for people over 50 *Born to Be Boomers*. It focuses on retirement, travel, health, and wellness. Tricia and Jack reside in Vero Beach, Florida, where they enjoy spending time with their children and three grandchildren.